TO:
FROM:
MESSAGE:

Published by Christian Art Publishers
PostNet Suite # 132, Private Bag X3706, Three Rivers, 1935,
South Africa

First edition 2023

Devotions compiled from
One-Minute Devotions® The Power of Prayer

Designed by Christian Art Publishers
Cover designed by Christian Art Publishers
Images used under license from Shutterstock.com

Printed in China

ISBN 978-0-638-00052-8

25 26 27 28 29 30 31 32 33 34 – 13 12 11 10 9 8 7 6 5 4

Mini Devotions

LIVING A LIFE OF PRAYER

E.M. BOUNDS

1

Wholeness through Prayer

But whatever were gains to me I now consider loss for the sake of Christ.

PHILIPPIANS 3:7

Prayer has to do with a person's whole being. When a person prays, he does so with his whole nature. When he receives benefits in prayer, it involves his whole being.

The largest results of praying come to him who gives himself—all of himself, all that belongs to himself—to God.

This is the secret of full consecration and the sort of praying that produces the largest fruit.

DEAR LORD, I want to give myself to You completely in prayer so that my life can produce the largest fruit for Your glory. Amen.

2

POWERFUL PRAYER

He will call on Me, and I will answer him; I will be with him in trouble, I will deliver him and honor him.

PSALM 91:15

What are the possibilities of prayer according to divine revelation? The necessity of prayer is coexistent with man. Nature cries out in prayer.

Man is; therefore, prayer is. God is; therefore, prayer is. Prayer is born of the instincts, the needs, the cravings, and the very being of man.

God put no limitation on His ability to save through true praying. The possibilities of prayer are linked to the infinite righteousness and to the omnipotent power of God. There is nothing too hard for God to do.

DEAR GOD, because all things are possible with You, I know that the possibilities of prayer are endless. All we have to do is ask. Amen.

3

Unite in Prayer

May God Himself, the God of peace, sanctify you through and through. May your whole spirit, soul and body be kept blameless at the coming of our Lord Jesus Christ.

1 THESSALONIANS 5:23

Holiness means wholeness. God wants holy people who are whole-hearted and true, for His service and for the work of praying. These are the sort of people God wants for leaders and these are the kind out of which the praying class is formed.

When a person prays every part of his being unites with God in prayer. Man unites in all the essentials and acts of piety. Soul, spirit, and body must unite in all things pertaining to life, holiness and godliness.

DEAR GOD, I want to be part of Your praying people. Make me whole and holy for Your service. Amen.

4

Kneeling to Pray

He withdrew about a stone's throw beyond them, knelt down and prayed.

LUKE 22:41

A person's body actively engages in prayer, since it assumes a specific position in prayer. Kneeling down of the body as well as the soul happens when someone prays. The attitude of the body counts much in prayer.

In Gethsemane our Lord prostrated Himself when He prayed just before His betrayal. Where there is earnest and faithful praying, the body always takes on the form most suited to the state of the soul at the time. In that way the body joins the soul in praying.

ALMIGHTY GOD, my soul is bent on pleasing You as my body kneels down before You in earnest prayer. Amen.

5

The Praying Mind

Do not conform to the pattern of this world, but be transformed by the renewing of your mind. Then you will be able to test and approve what God's will is—His good, pleasing and perfect will.

ROMANS 12:2

The whole being of a person must engage in prayer. A person's life, heart, temper and mind should be in it. Every fiber of a person should join in the prayer exercise.

A person's intellect must also add energy when praying. Necessarily the mind plays a role in prayer. First of all, one thinks about praying. The intellect teaches us that we ought to pray. By serious thinking beforehand, the mind prepares itself for approaching the throne of grace.

Thought precedes entering into prayer and prepares the way; it considers what will be asked in prayer.

DEAR GOD, as I approach Your throne of grace I want to give my all to You–body, mind and soul. Amen.

6

Just Asking

"Lord, teach us to pray."

LUKE 11:1

True praying involves knowing beforehand what to request from God. Praying is asking for something definite. The mind is given over entirely to God, thinking of Him, of what is needed, and of what has been received in the past.

The very first step in prayer is a mental step. We must be taught through our intellect. And only as far as the intellect is given over to God in prayer will we be able to learn how to pray.

LORD JESUS, just like Your disciples long ago I ask of You today, "teach us to pray." Amen.

7

THE DIVINE ASPECT

Now faith is confidence in what we hope for and assurance about what we do not see.

HEBREWS 11:1

Often, earnestness is mistaken for anointing. He who has the divine anointing will be earnest in the spiritual nature of things.

Earnestness may mean being sincere, serious, ardent, and persevering. But all these forces cannot rise higher than the mere human. The man is in it—the whole man, but God might not be in it. Earnestness could be selfishness in disguise.

What about the anointing? It is the indefinable aspect of preaching which makes it preaching. Anointing is that which distinguishes and separates preaching from all mere human speeches and presentations. It is the divine aspect in preaching.

DEAR GOD, when I come to You in prayer I want to pray selflessly, and that by Your grace I may receive the anointing of Your Holy Spirit. Please guide me. Amen.

8

Far-Reaching Prayer

Blessed are they who keep His statutes and seek Him with all their heart.

PSALM 119:2

It is godly people who give themselves entirely over to prayer. Prayer is far-reaching in its influence and in its gracious effects.

It is an intense and profound business that deals with God and His plans and purposes, and it takes whole-hearted people to do it.

No half-hearted, half-spirited effort will do for this all-important, heavenly business. The whole person must be engaged in the matter of praying which so mightily affects the characters and destinies of those who pray.

DEAR LORD GOD, when I pray I know that no half-hearted, half-spirited effort will do. Please help me to surrender my all to You in prayer. Amen.

9

TODAY'S MANNA

You will keep in perfect peace those whose minds are steadfast, because they trust in You.

ISAIAH 26:3

True prayers are born out of present trials and needs. Bread received today is the strongest pledge that there will be bread tomorrow. We must trust God today and leave tomorrow entirely with Him. The present is ours; the future belongs to God.

As every day demands its bread, so every day demands its prayer. No amount of praying done today will be sufficient for tomorrow's praying.

Today's manna is what we need; tomorrow God will see that our needs are supplied. This is the faith that God seeks to inspire. So leave tomorrow with its cares and troubles in God's hands.

DEAR GOD, please help me to trust You for today's needs and to leave tomorrow entirely in Your hands. I know You will provide. Amen.

10

THE PRAYING CHRISTIAN

I urge you, brothers and sisters, by our Lord Jesus Christ and by the love of the Spirit, to join me in my struggle by praying to God for me.

ROMANS 15:30

Paul knew how to pray with his whole being. The words "to join me in my struggle" tell of Paul's praying and how much he put into it. It is like a great battle. Like a soldier, the praying Christian fights a life-and-death battle. His honor and eternal life are all at stake. Everything depends on the strength he puts in it.

Just as it involves every part of a person's complex being to pray successfully, so in turn the person receives the benefits of such praying. This kind of praying engages our undivided hearts, our full consent to be the Lord's.

DEAR GOD, I want to thank You for knowing that when we pray to You with our whole being, You will bless our entire lives. Amen.

11

A Gracious Touch

He makes me lie down in green pastures, He leads me beside quiet waters, He refreshes my soul. He guides me along the right paths for His name's sake.

PSALM 23:2-3

God sees to it that when every part of a believer prays, He blesses that person. Clear thinking, an enlightened understanding, and safe reasoning powers come from praying.

Divine guidance means that God moves and impresses the mind in order for us to make wise decisions. Many praying preachers have been greatly helped and guided by God just at this point. In former days, when men of very limited education had such wonderful liberty of invigorated minds and thoughts from the Spirit, they explained it as successful prayer. Their minds felt the impulse of the Spirit's gracious influences.

DEAR GOD, I pray that Your divine guidance will lead me in such a way that I, too, will be able to experience the Spirit's gracious touch upon my life. Amen.

12

To Have Faith

"Truly I tell you, if anyone says to this mountain, 'Go, throw yourself into the sea,' and does not doubt in their heart but believes that what they say will happen, it will be done for them."

MARK 11:23

Faith is the essential quality in the heart of any believer who desires to communicate effectively with God.

He must believe and stretch out the hands of faith to that which cannot be seen. Prayer is faith claiming and taking hold of its natural, immeasurable inheritance. Moreover, when faith ceases to pray, it ceases to live.

Faith does the impossible because it lets God undertake for us, and nothing is impossible with God. How great—without qualification or limitation—is the power of faith!

ALMIGHTY GOD, if I want to communicate with You effectively, faith is the essential quality. Thank You that the impossible is possible with You. Amen.

13

When Faith Fails

"Simon, Simon, Satan has asked to sift all of you as wheat. But I have prayed for you, Simon, that your faith may not fail. And when you have turned back, strengthen your brothers."

LUKE 22:31-32

Faith is the foundation of a Christian character and the security of the soul. Here Jesus was looking toward Peter's denial and cautioning him against it. Our Lord was stating a central truth. It was Peter's faith He was seeking to guard.

He knew that when faith breaks down, the foundations of spiritual life give way too, and the entire structure of religious experience falls.

It was Peter's faith that needed guarding. That is why Christ was concerned for the welfare of His disciple's soul and was determined to strengthen Peter's faith through His own victorious prayer.

GOD, You know that when our faith fails, our spiritual lives give way. Please strengthen and guard my faith today so that my eyes will be fixed on You always. Amen.

14

Adding Grace to Grace

For this very reason, make every effort to add to your faith goodness; and to goodness, knowledge; and to knowledge, self-control; and to self-control, perseverance; and to perseverance, godliness.

2 PETER 1:5-6

Growing in grace and fruitfulness is a measure of safety in the Christian life. Faith is the starting point, the basis of the other graces of the Holy Spirit. To grow in grace depends on starting right.

There is a divine order and Peter was aware of it. He went on to say that we should give constant care to making our calling and election secure. This election is secured by adding to faith that which is done by constant, earnest praying. Faith is kept alive by prayer. Every step in this adding of grace to grace is accompanied by prayer.

DEAR GOD, I want to grow in grace and faith. Please guide me through Your Holy Spirit to strengthen my faith through constant prayer. Amen.

15

Powerful Praying

Then Jesus came to them and said, "All authority in heaven and on earth has been given to Me."

MATTHEW 28:18

Faith that creates powerful praying is the faith that centers around a powerful Person. Faith in Christ's ability to *do* and to do greatly, is the faith that prays greatly.

It was because He wanted to inspire faith in His ability to do that Jesus left that last, great statement behind for us as a ringing challenge to our faith.

Faith is obedient. It goes when commanded, as did the nobleman who came to Jesus when his son was grievously sick. To do God's will is essential to true faith, and faith is necessary for absolute obedience.

DEAR LORD, please help me to put my trust in You more every day so that my faith may increase to pray more effectively and powerfully to You. Amen.

16

Patient Faith

Be still before the Lord and wait patiently for Him.
PSALM 37:7

Faith often requires waiting patiently before God and being prepared to wait for His seeming delays in answering prayer. Faith does not grow disheartened because prayer is not immediately answered. It takes God at His word and lets Him take what time He chooses in fulfilling His purposes and in carrying out His work.

There is bound to be some delays and long days of waiting for true faith, but faith accepts the conditions. It knows there will be delays in answering prayer and regards such delays as times of testing where it is privileged to show that it is made of courage and perseverance.

DEAR GOD, please help me to wait patiently for Your answers to my prayers. Thank You that because of my faith in You, I will not grow disheartened. Amen.

17

Today's Fresh Bread

"Give us today our daily bread."

MATTHEW 6:11

Faith covers worldly as well as spiritual needs. Faith drives away anxiety and unnecessary worries about what you will eat, what you will drink and what you will wear. Faith brings great peace of mind and perfect peace of heart.

When we pray for our "daily bread", we are in fact shutting tomorrow out of our prayers. We do not look for tomorrow's grace or bread.

Those who pray best pray for today's, not tomorrow's needs. Our prayers for tomorrow's needs may be unnecessary because tomorrow might not exist at all!

FATHER GOD, I know that You will provide for Your children day by day. That is why I pray only for today's bread. Amen.

18

PRAYING IS NO EASY TASK

He answered, "'Love the Lord your God with all your heart and with all your soul and with all your strength and with all your mind'; and, 'Love your neighbor as yourself.'"

LUKE 10:27

This was the answer of Jesus to the scribe as to what was the first and greatest commandment. In other words, the whole person must love the Father God without reservation. Such a person is required to do the praying that God asks of His children.

Just as it requires a whole heart given to God to gladly and fully obey God's commandments, so it takes a whole heart to pray effectively. And because it requires the whole person to pray, praying is no easy task. Praying is far more than simply bending the knee and saying a few random words. Praying is divine.

LORD, I realize again today that prayer is no easy task. You ask all of me when I come to You in prayer. Please help me pray. Amen.

19

The Dedication of the Temple

"Now my eyes will be open and my ears attentive to the prayers offered in this place. I have chosen and consecrated this temple so that My Name may be there forever."

2 CHRONICLES 7:15-16

Solomon's prayer at the dedication of the temple is the product of inspired wisdom and piety, and it gives a lucid and powerful view of prayer. National calamities, sins, damage to crops as well as individual needs such as sickness, pain and one's own sin are in this prayer.

For all these things, prayer is the one universal remedy. Prayer to God, pure praying, relieves dire situations because God can relieve when no one else can. Nothing is too difficult for God.

ALMIGHTY GOD, thank You that I know You can do all things and that You can relieve all the troubles in my life. I only have to pray earnestly to You. Amen.

20

A Growing Faith

"Therefore I tell you, whatever you ask for in prayer, believe that you have received it, and it will be yours."

MARK 11:24

Prayer puts faith in God and moves God's hand in the world. Only God can move mountains, but faith and prayer move God. In the cursing of the fig tree, our Lord demonstrated His power. Following that, He went on to say that large powers were committed to faith and prayer, not to kill but to make alive.

A faith that makes things happen is described here. This faith is an awareness of God, an experienced communion, a fact.

Is faith growing or declining as the years go by? Does faith stand strong and firm as sin abounds and the love of many grows cold?

LORD, it is only You who can move mountains, but thank You that my faith and my prayers move You. I praise Your name. Amen.

21

Times of Trouble

"And call on Me in the day of trouble; I will deliver you, and you will honor Me."

PSALM 50:15

The many statements in God's Word set forth the possibilities and far-reaching nature and effects of prayer.

Yet the range of prayer is as great as trouble, as universal as sorrow and as infinite as grief. And prayer can relieve all these evils that come to God's people. There is no tear that prayer cannot wipe away. There is no depression of spirit that it cannot elevate. There is no despair that it cannot dispel.

Prayer always brings God to our relief to bless and to aid, and it brings marvelous revelations of His power.

LORD GOD, I know that in this life we will have troubles. But thank You that we can know that we don't have to lose heart, because You have overcome this world. Amen.

22

SAMUEL, MAN OF PRAYER

"As for me, far be it from me that I should sin against the LORD by failing to pray for you."

1 SAMUEL 12:23

Samuel stands out in the Old Testament as one of the men who had great influence with God through prayer. God could not deny him anything he asked for. Samuel's praying always affected God and moved God to do what would not have otherwise been done had he not prayed. Samuel stands out as a striking illustration of the possibilities of prayer. Prayer was no strange exercise to Samuel.

Through him and his praying, God's cause was brought out of its low, depressed condition. A great national revival began, of which David was one of its fruits.

GOD, thank You that You use ordinary people, equip them, and guide them to do great things for Your glory. Amen.

23

The School of Delay

Truly, truly, I say to you, we speak of what we know, and bear witness to what we have seen; but you do not receive our testimony.

JOHN 3:11 RSV

Delay is often the test and the strength of faith; yet faith gathers strength by waiting and praying. Patience is learned best when waiting is required. In some instances, delay is of the very nature of prayer.

God has to do many things before He gives the final answer. Things that are essential to the lasting good of the person who is requesting the favor from Him.

Fear not, Jesus will come. His delay will serve to make His coming more richly blessed. Keep on praying. Keep on waiting. He will come and will not be late.

DEAR GOD, I praise Your name and I thank You that I can be sure of Your answers to my prayers. Even as I wait, I know You will never be late. Amen.

24

The Divine Art of Preaching

They asked each other, "Were not our hearts burning within us while he talked with us on the road and opened the Scriptures to us?"

LUKE 24:32

The preacher who has lost this anointing has lost the art of preaching.

Whatever other talents or abilities he may have and retain—the art of sermon making, the art of eloquence, the art of great, clear thinking, the art of pleasing an audience—he has lost the divine art of preaching. This anointing makes God's truth powerful and interesting; it draws, attracts, edifies, convicts and saves.

This same anointing vitalizes God's revealed truth and makes it life-giving. Just like God's truth spoken without this anointing is dead.

GOD, I pray for Your anointing on my life today so that I, too, can bring Your message to other people in a powerful way. Amen.

25

Praying in the Name of Jesus

"You may ask Me for anything in My name, and I will do it."

JOHN 14:14

What a wonderful statement! What God will do in answer to prayer in His name! Faith in Jesus Christ is the basis of all working and all praying.

All wonderful works depend on wonderful praying, and all praying is done in the name of Jesus Christ. The amazing, simple lesson is to pray in the name of the Lord Jesus! All other conditions are of little value.

If Jesus dwells in your heart—if the flow of His life has replaced all of your life—then absolute obedience to Him is the inspiration and force of every movement of your life.

LORD, thank You that we may ask for anything in Your name, and You will do it. Amen.

26

THE ENERGY OF GOD

For Christ's love compels us, because we are convinced that one died for all, and therefore all died.
2 CORINTHIANS 5:14

Divine anointing is the feature that distinguishes true gospel preaching from all other methods of presenting the Truth. It supports revealed truth with all the energy of God.

Anointing is simply allowing God to be in His own Word and on His own people. It inspires and clarifies a person's intellect, gives insight and projects power. It gives the preacher heart-power which is greater than head-power.

Growth, fullness of thought, and simplicity of preaching are the fruits of this anointing.

DEAR LORD JESUS, I pray for Your divine anointing to inspire my intellect, give me insight and reveal Your power through me. In Jesus' name I pray. Amen.

27

God-Like Sympathies

For there is one God and one mediator between God and mankind, the man Christ Jesus, who gave Himself as a ransom for all people.

1 TIMOTHY 2:5-6

Paul knew that the nature of prayer is part of a person's being. It must be so. It takes the whole man to embrace in its godlike sympathies the entire race of man—the sorrows and the sins of all people.

It takes the whole man to run parallel with God's high will in saving mankind. It takes the whole man to stand with our Lord Jesus Christ as the Mediator between God and sinful people.

It takes a whole person to pray, until all the storms that agitate his soul are calmed to great tranquility.

DEAR LORD JESUS I want to thank You that You came to be the Mediator between God and us. Thank You that You gave Yourself as a ransom for our sins. Amen.

28

THE GIFT OF GOD

Let us draw near to God with a sincere heart and with the full assurance that faith brings, having our hearts sprinkled to cleanse us from a guilty conscience and having our bodies washed with pure water.

HEBREWS 10:22

This anointing comes to the preacher not in the study of God's Word, but in spending time with God. It is heaven's distillation in answer to prayer. It carries the Word like dynamite. It makes the hearer a culprit or a saint—makes him weep like a child and live like a giant.

It opens his heart and his purse as gently, yet as strongly as the spring opens the leaves. This anointing is not the gift of genius. It is the gift of God. It is heaven's knighthood given to the brave ones who have sought this anointed honor through many hours of prayer.

GOD, I draw near to You with a sincere heart. Please open my heart for Your divine gifts. In Jesus' name. Amen.

29

WONDERFUL TRUST

"Do not let your hearts be troubled. You believe in God; believe also in Me."

JOHN 14:1

Prayer does not stand alone. It lives in fellowship with other Christian duties. Prayer is firmly joined to faith. Faith gives it color and tone, and secures its results.

Trust is faith accomplished. Trust is a conscious act, a fact of which we are aware. It is the feeling of the soul—the spiritual sight, hearing and taste.

All these have to do with trust. How bright, distinct, conscious, powerful, and scriptural such a trust is!

DEAR GOD, I put my trust in You all day long. Amen.

30

Prayer Set on Fire

Devote yourselves to prayer, being watchful and thankful.

COLOSSIANS 4:2

The Holy Spirit came as our promised Comforter, to help us in our prayer lives. The Holy Spirit's coming is not conditioned on a little process and a mere performance of prayer, but on prayer set on fire by an unquenchable desire.

This prayer must be accompanied by such a sense of need that it cannot be denied, and by a fixed determination that will not let go and that will never fail until it secures the best and last blessing God has in store for us.

DEAR FATHER, I thank You for sending us Your Holy Spirit to comfort us and guide our prayer lives. Amen.

31

Waiting in Prayer

Then Jesus said to her, "Woman, you have great faith! Your request is granted." And her daughter was healed at that moment.

MATTHEW 15:28

Trust brings eternity into the history and happen of time. Trust sees, receives, holds. Trust is its own witness. But quite often, faith is too weak to obtain God's greatest good immediately. It has to wait in loving obedience, until it grows in strength and is able to bring down the eternal into the areas of experience and time.

Up to this point, trust is the deciding factor. In faith's struggle to grow stronger, trust also increases. If we trust in God, we will become more aware of all the good things that He has done for us.

While waiting in prayer, faith rises to its highest level and becomes the gift of God. It becomes a constant fellowship with a tireless request to God.

ALMIGHTY GOD, I know that if I trust in You, You will grant my requests. Thank You, Lord. Amen.

32

THE EYE OF TRUST

As Scripture says, "Anyone who believes in Him will never be put to shame."

ROMANS 10:11

Trust grows richly when a person prays in solitude. When a person's quiet time with God is sincere, trust grows increasingly. The eye and the presence of God give active life to trust, just like the eye and presence of the sun make fruit and flowers grow.

Faith and trust in the Lord form the keynote and foundation of prayer. Primarily, it is not trust in the Word of God, but rather trust in the person of God. For trust in the person of God must precede trust in the Word of God.

The person of Jesus Christ must be central to the eye of trust.

DEAR GOD, You are the central point of trust in my life. Please make my trust grow as I come to You in prayer. Amen.

Believe without a Doubt

The apostles said to the Lord, "Increase our faith!"
LUKE 17:5 RSV

Do we believe without a doubt? When we pray, do we believe that we will receive the things we ask for, not on a future day, but then and there? This is not so easy. The ability to believe without doubting is only reached after many failures and much trial of faith.

Our Lord puts forth trust as the very foundation of praying. The background of prayer is trust. The whole purpose of Christ's ministry and work was dependent on absolute trust in His Father. The center of trust is God.

Mountains of difficulties and all other hindrances to prayer are moved out of the way by trust and its strong follower, faith.

FATHER GOD, thank You that You can move mountains if we only trust and believe in You. I praise Your holy name. Amen.

34

The Outstretched Hand

"According to your faith let it be done to you"; and their sight was restored.

MATTHEW 9:29-30

When trust is perfect and there is no doubt, prayer is simply the outstretched hand ready to receive. Trust perfected is prayer perfected. Trust looks to receive the thing asked for and gets it. Trust is not a belief that God can bless or that He will bless, but that He does bless, here and now.

Trust always operates in the present tense. Hope looks toward the future. Trust looks to the present. Hope expects. Trust possesses. Trust receives what prayer acquires. So, what prayer needs, at all times, is abiding and abundant trust.

DEAR LORD, my prayers still need more abiding and abundant trust so that I can receive all the blessings from Your hand. Please guide me in my trust today. Amen.

35

THE SIMPLICITY OF TRUST

The word is near you; it is in your mouth and in your heart.

ROMANS 10:8

When people came to Him, our Lord put their trust in Him and the divinity of His mission in the forefront. He did not give a definition of trust. He knew that men would see what faith was by what faith did. They would see from its free exercise that trust grew, automatically, in His presence.

It was the product of His work, His power, and His person. Trust is too simple for verbal definition. It is too sincere and spontaneous for theological terms. The very simplicity of trust is what astounds many people.

DEAR FATHER GOD, I know that trust grows in Your presence. Thank You that I can know what faith is by what faith can do. Amen.

36

FOR SACRED USE

He and all his family were devout and God-fearing; he gave generously to those in need and prayed to God regularly.

ACTS 10:2

Devotion has great religious significance. The root meaning of devotion is "to devote to a sacred use." Thus, devotion, in its true sense, has to do with religious worship. It stands intimately connected with true prayer. Devotion is the particular frame of mind found in a person entirely devoted to God. It is the spirit of reverence and godly fear. It is a state of heart that appears before God in prayer and worship.

It is unfamiliar with things like lightness of spirit and is opposed to noise and complaining. Devotion dwells in the realm of quietness and is still before God. It is thoughtful, serious and meditative.

ALMIGHTY GOD, I devote myself to Your sacred use today. I come to You in quietness and stillness of heart, please speak to me today. Amen.

37

His Chosen Agents

A man named Ananias came to see me. He was a devout observer of the law and highly respected by all the Jews living there.

ACTS 22:12

Devotion is a part of the very spirit of true worship and is of the nature of the spirit of prayer. Devotion belongs to the person whose thoughts and feelings are devoted to God. Such a person has a mind given up wholly to religion and possesses a strong affection for God and a passionate love for His house.

God can wonderfully use dedicated people, for they are His chosen agents in carrying forward His plans.

DEAR GOD, I devote my feelings and thoughts to You and I give myself wholly up to Your purposes. As Your chosen agent I want to carry Your plans forward. Amen.

38

THE LITTLE THINGS OF LIFE

Do not be anxious about anything, but in every situation, by prayer and petition, with thanksgiving, present your requests to God.

PHILIPPIANS 4:6

The possibilities of prayer are to be seen in its accomplishments in earthly matters. Prayer reaches to everything that concerns people, whether it be the body, the mind or the soul.

Prayer takes in the needs of the body, such as food and clothes, and concerns itself with business and finances—in fact everything that belongs to this life, as well as those things that have to do with the eternal interests of the soul.

The achievements of prayer are seen not only in the large things but also in the small things.

DEAR LORD, I thank You for Your hand in the important earthly matters, but also for Your presence in the little things of life. Amen.

39

Our Health and Happiness

I pray that you may enjoy good health and that all may go well with you, even as your soul is getting along well.

3 JOHN 2

Earthly matters are of a lower order than the spiritual, but they concern us greatly. They are the main source of our cares and worries. They have much to do with our religion. We have bodies with needs, pains, disabilities and limitations. That which concerns our bodies necessarily engages our minds. These are subjects of prayer.

Earthly matters also greatly impact our health and happiness. They form our relations. If we do not pray about worldly matters we exclude God from a large area of our lives.

FATHER GOD, it is my desire to include You in every sphere of my life. Thank You for caring about our earthly needs and pains. Amen.

40

Worldly Matters

"Give us today our daily bread."

MATTHEW 6:11

To leave business and time out of prayer is to leave religion and eternity out of it. He who does not pray about worldly matters cannot pray with confidence about spiritual matters.

He who does not put God in his struggling toil for daily bread will never put Him in his struggle for heaven. He who does not cover and supply the needs of the body by prayer will never cover and supply the needs of his soul.

Both body and soul are dependent on God, and prayer is but the crying expression of that dependence.

ALMIGHTY GOD, my body and my soul yearn for You. I praise Your name for supplying my earthly and my spiritual needs. Amen.

41

GOD CARES

Cast all your anxiety on Him, for He cares about you.

1 PETER 5:7 RSV

Prayer enables us to carry all our worries to God in prayer and if we doubt when we pray we upset our hearts unnecessarily.

How much needless care would we save ourselves if we just believed in prayer as the means of relieving those cares, and would learn the happy art of casting all our cares in prayer upon God, who cares for us!

Disbelief that God is concerned about even the smallest affairs that affect our happiness and comfort limits the Holy One of Israel and makes our lives altogether devoid of real happiness.

DEAR GOD, I cast all my anxieties on You today, for You care about the smallest affairs of my life. Thank You for loving me. Amen.

42

An Absent Heart

"These people come near to Me with their mouth and honor Me with their lips, but their hearts are far from Me."

ISAIAH 29:13

Devotion engages the heart in prayer. It is not an easy task for the lips to try to pray while the heart is absent from it. The very essence of prayer is the spirit of devotion.

Without devotion, prayer is empty, a vain round of words. Sad to say, much of this kind of prayer prevails in the church today. This is a busy age, bustling and active, and this bustling spirit has invaded the church of God. Its religious performances are many.

True worship finds congeniality in the heart and spirit of devotion.

LORD, I want to engage all of me when I come to You in prayer. Please give me a heart and spirit of devotion so that I can truly worship You. Amen.

43

YOUR WHOLE HEART

Do not conform to the pattern of this world, but be transformed by the renewing of your mind. Then you will be able to test and approve what God's will is—His good, pleasing and perfect will.

ROMANS 12:2

Religion engages our hands and feet, it takes hold of our voices, it lays its hands on our money, it affects even the postures of our bodies. But it does not take hold of our affections, our desires, and cause us to worship in the presence of God.

Church membership can sometimes become a facade of respectable behavior that does not involve our hearts. It remains cold and unimpressed among all this outward performance, while we congratulate ourselves that we are doing wonderfully well religiously. Put your whole heart into your religion today, not just appearance!

DEAR FATHER, please renew my heart and mind so that I may know Your good, pleasing and perfect will for my life. Amen.

44

To Handle Things Sacredly

For in Him we live and move and have our being. As some of your own poets have said, "We are His offspring."

ACTS 17:28

Religion sometimes lacks the spirit of devotion. We hear sermons in the same spirit with which we listen to a lecture or hear a speech. We visit the house of God just as if it were a common place; like the theater or lecture hall.

We look upon the pastor of God not as the divinely called man of God, but merely as a sort of public speaker. We handle sacred things as if they were the things of the world.

Oh, how a spirit of genuine devotion would radically change all this for the better!

ALMIGHTY GOD, I pray that You will open my heart for Your voice and give me a spirit of devotion for Your sacred work on earth. Amen.

45

Common Things Sacred

So whether you eat or drink or whatever you do, do it all for the glory of God.

1 CORINTHIANS 10:31

We need the spirit of devotion, not only to be the salt in our worldly activities, but to make our prayers real prayers. We need to put the spirit of devotion into Monday's business as well as in Sunday's worship.

We need the spirit of devotion to recollect the presence of God and direct all things to His glory. The spirit of devotion puts God in all things. It puts God not just in our praying and churchgoing, but in all the aspects of life. The spirit of devotion makes the common things of earth sacred, and the little things great.

DEAR LORD, I want to do everything for Your glory. I need a spirit of devotion to make my prayers real. Please guide me. Amen.

46

A Sabbath on Saturday

In the same way, faith by itself, if it is not accompanied by action, is dead.

JAMES 2:17

With a spirit of devotion to do all things for God's glory, we go to the workplace on Monday. Directed and inspired by the very same influence we went to church with on Sunday. The spirit of devotion makes a Sabbath out of Saturday and transforms the shop or the office into a temple of God.

The spirit of devotion removes religion from being a thin veneer and puts it into our souls. With devotion in our soul, religion stops merely doing a work and becomes a heart, beating with the pulsations of vigorous and radiant life.

DEAR LORD GOD, through a spirit of devotion I can bring glory to Your name. Please grant me a heart beating with vigor for You. Amen.

47

THE AROMA OF RELIGION

Dear friends, now we are children of God, and what we will be has not yet been made known. But we know that when Christ appears, we shall be like Him, for we shall see Him as He is.

1 JOHN 3:2

The spirit of devotion is not merely the aroma of religion, but the stalk and stem on which religion grows. It dispels idleness, and makes worship a serious and deep-rooted service that fills body, soul and spirit with a heavenly infusion.

Let us ask in all honesty: Has this highest angel of heaven, this heavenly spirit of devotion, this brightest and best angel of earth, left us? When the angel of devotion has gone, the angel of prayer has lost its wings, and it becomes a deformed and loveless thing. Never let the stalk and stem of your religion die. Water your spirit of devotion daily.

GOD, I pray for the heavenly spirit of devotion to return to my life so that I may worship You with new spiritual fervor. Amen.

48

Devotion Reacts to Prayer

Let everything that has breath praise the Lord. Praise the Lord.

PSALM 150:6

Prayer promotes the spirit of devotion while devotion is an important aspect of effective prayer. It is easy to pray when you are in a spirit of devotion. God dwells where the spirit of devotion resides. Indeed, these graces grow nowhere else but here.

The absence of a devoted spirit means death to the graces born in a renewed heart. True worship finds kindness in the atmosphere of a spirit of devotion. While prayer is helpful to devotion, at the same time devotion reacts to prayer and helps us to pray.

DEAR FATHER, where my spirit of devotion is there You are also. Thank You, Lord. Amen.

49

The Passion of Devotion

Day and night they never stop saying: "Holy, holy, holy is the Lord God Almighty, who was, and is, and is to come."

REVELATION 4:8

The passion of devotion lies in prayer. The spirit of devotion fills the hearts of God's children and characterizes their worship. The inspiration and center of their joyful devotion is the holiness of God. That holiness of God claims their attention and inflames their devotion.

There is nothing cold, nothing dull, nothing lifeless about them or their heavenly worship. What zeal! The ministry of prayer, if it be anything worthy of the name, is a ministry of passion, a ministry of intense longing after God and His holiness.

FATHER GOD, I long to be in Your presence, singing praises with a spirit of passion and devotion to You. Amen.

50

Prayer Must Be Aflame

Then I saw a new heaven and a new earth, for the first heaven and the first earth had passed away. And I heard a loud voice from the throne saying, "God's dwelling place is now among the people, and He will dwell with them. They will be His people, and God Himself will be with them and be their God."

REVELATION 21:1, 3

There are no creatures without devotion in heaven. God is there, and His very presence results in a spirit of reverence. If we would join them in heaven after death, we must first learn the spirit of devotion on earth before we get there.

These living creatures are the perfect examples and illustrations of true prayer. Prayer must be aflame. Prayer without fervor is like a sun without light or heat. Only he who glows for God can truly pray.

ALMIGHTY GOD, please set my soul aflame with fervor for You so that I may shine brightly for all the world to see. Amen.

51

Actions without Devotion

My God will meet all your needs according to the riches of His glory in Christ Jesus.

PHILIPPIANS 4:19

Work is not zeal. Moving about is not devotion. Activity is often the unrecognized symptom of spiritual weakness. It may be hurtful to piety when actions are made the substitute for real devotion in worship. The child is more active than the father, who may be bearing the rule and burdens of an empire on his heart and shoulders. Enthusiasm is more active than faith, though it cannot call into action any of the omnipotent forces that faith can command.

If your spiritual life is real, a deep-toned activity will spring from it. It is an activity springing from strength and not from weakness.

FATHER, I don't want my actions to be without devotion and zeal. I want my spiritual life to be real so that my activities will glorify You. Amen.

52

The Flower and Fruit of a Holy Life

His divine power has given us everything we need for a godly life through our knowledge of Him who called us by His own glory and goodness.

2 PETER 1:3

In the nature of things, religion must show much of its growth above ground. The flower and fruit of a holy life, abounding in good works, must be seen. It cannot be otherwise. But the surface growth must be based on a vigorous growth of unseen life and hidden roots.

The roots of religion must go down deep in the renewed nature to be seen on the outside. There should be much of the invisible and the underground growth, or else the life will be feeble and short-lived, and the external growth fruitless.

LORD, I want to bear the fruit of Your Spirit in my life. Please make my roots grow ever deeper. Amen.

53

Too Busy

"But those who hope in the Lord will renew their strength. They will soar on wings like eagles; they will run and not grow weary..."

ISAIAH 40:31

To run and not grow weary is the beginning of the whole matter of activity and strength. All this is the result of waiting on God.

There may be lots of activities created by enthusiasm. Activity often continues at the expense of more solid, useful elements and generally to the total neglect of prayer. To be too busy with God's work to commune with Him, to be busy with doing church work without taking time to talk to God about His work, is the highway to backsliding. In spite of great activity, the work will be helpless without the cultivation and the maturity of the graces of prayer.

FATHER GOD, please help me not to become so busy with Your work that I don't take time to consult with You about what You want me to do. Amen.

54

A Life with Feeling

"Therefore I tell you, whatever you ask for in prayer, believe that you have received it, and it will be yours."

MARK 11:24

Trust, like life, is feeling. An unfelt life is a contradiction in terms. Trust is the most felt of all qualities. It is all feeling, and it only works by love. An unfelt love is as impossible as an unfelt trust.

The trust we are speaking about is a conviction. Trust sees God doing things here and now. It transforms hope into the reality of fulfillment and changes promise into present possession.

We know when we trust, just as we know when we see. Trust sees, receives, holds. Trust is its own witness.

DEAR GOD, thank You that our trust in You transforms our hope into fulfilled realities. You are wonderful God. Amen.

55

THE GOLDEN RULE—PRAYER

"He has shown you, O mortal, what is good. To act justly and to love mercy and to walk humbly with your God."

MICAH 6:8

The ministry of prayer has been the special distinction of all God's saints. The energy and the soul of their work have come from their prayer lives.

Because the need for help outside of man is so great—given man's natural inability to always judge kindly, justly, and truly and to act out the Golden Rule—prayer is instructed by Christ to enable man to act in all these things according to His divine will. By prayer, the ability is secured to feel the law of love, to speak according to the law of love, and to do everything in harmony with God's law of love.

LORD GOD, You gave prayer to us so that through Christ we are able to do all things for Your glory. I want to walk in harmony with Your law of love. Amen.

56

A Current of Prayer

We will give our attention to prayer and the ministry of the word.

ACTS 6:4

Prayer must be incessant and should not lack desire, spirit or action. The knees may not always be bent, but the spirit is always in the act and communication of prayer.

The spirit of prayer should sweetly rule and adjust all times and occasions. Our activities and work should be performed in the same spirit that makes our devotion and our prayer time sacred.

Blessed is the person of God who thus understands prayer, at any point, at any time. A full current of prayer is seen flowing from him.

DEAR FATHER, I want my spirit to always be bent to You in prayer, even when I'm not on my knees. Amen.

57

Trust from the Heart

Trust in the Lord.

PSALM 37:3

The trust in history or records may be a passive thing, but trust in a person strengthens the quality. The trust that supplies prayer centers in a Person.

Trust goes even further than this. The trust that inspires our prayer must not only be in the Person of God, and of Christ, but in their ability and willingness to grant the things we pray for. And to trust that, as our Lord taught, a condition of effective prayer is not from the head but from the heart.

The strong promise of our Lord brings faith down to the present and counts on a present answer.

DEAR LORD, I believe that by trusting in You, You will grant us the desires of our hearts. I praise Your name. Amen.

58

Prayer and Desire

The prayer of a righteous person is powerful and effective.

JAMES 5:16

To desire something is not merely a simple wish. In the realm of spiritual affairs, it is so important that one could almost say desire is an absolute essential of prayer. Desire precedes and accompanies prayer. Prayer is the verbal expression of desire. Prayer comes out into the open. Desire is silent. Prayer is heard. The deeper the desire, the stronger the prayer.

Without desire, prayer is a meaningless mumble of words. Such uninterested, formal praying, with no heart, feeling, or real desire, is to be avoided like a plague. Its exercise is a waste of precious time, and no real blessing results from it.

DEAR GOD, all that I desire is to worship You. Please guide me that my prayers will be accompanied by a strong desire to do Your will. Amen.

59

Where Grace Abounds, Song Abounds

Let the peoples praise Thee, O God.

PSALM 67:5 RSV

When God is in a person's heart, heaven is present and melody is found there. This is as true in the private life of the believer as it is in the congregations of the saints. The decay of singing means the decline of grace in the heart and the absence of God's presence from the people.

The main purpose of singing is for God's ear; to attract His attention and to please Him. Certainly it is not for the glorification of the paid choir, nor to draw people to the church, but it is for the glory of God and the good of the souls of the congregation.

FATHER GOD, I want to sing praises to Your name. I want to glorify and please You with my song, for You have been good to me. Amen.

60

Love Grows as Gratitude Grows

Because He turned His ear to me, I will call on Him as long as I live.

PSALM 116:2

Love is the child of gratitude. Love grows as gratitude is felt and then breaks out into praise and thanksgiving to God. Answered prayers cause gratitude, and gratitude brings forth a love that declares to never stop praying. Gratitude and love move to larger and increased prayer.

Consideration of God's mercies not only creates gratitude, but leads to a large consecration to God of all that we have and are. Thus, prayer, thanksgiving, and consecration are all inseparably linked together.

DEAR LORD GOD, I praise You because I have been fearfully and wonderfully made. Thank You for loving me. Amen.

61

Heavenly Appetites

"Blessed are those who hunger and thirst for righteousness, for they will be filled."

MATTHEW 5:6

Heaven-given appetites are proof of a renewed heart and the evidence of a stirring spiritual life. Spiritual desires belong to a soul made alive to God. As the renewed soul hungers and thirsts after righteousness, these holy desires break out into prayer.

In prayer we are dependent on the name and power of Jesus to satisfy our hunger for Him. The vital basis of prayer is seated in the human heart. It is not simply our need; it is the heart's desire for what we need and for what we feel urged to pray about. Desire is the will in action.

FATHER, my soul thirsts and hungers after You. Thank You for satisfying my every need. Amen.

62

Burning Desire

You say, "I am rich; I have acquired wealth and do not need a thing." But you do not realize that you are wretched, pitiful, poor, blind and naked.

REVELATION 3:17

It is impossible to ask whether the feebleness of our desire for our heavenly Father is the cause of our lack of prayer. Do we really feel this inward hunger for heavenly treasures? No, the fire burns entirely too low. This, we should remember, was the major cause of the sad condition of the Laodicean Christians.

Our hearts need to be renewed, not only to get the evil out of them, but to get the good into them too. They need to be renewed so that the inspiration to turn toward heavenly things is a strong, moving desire.

DEAR GOD, sometimes my feeble desire is the reason for my lack of prayer. Please create in me a pure heart and renew the right spirit within me. Amen.

63

Visible Thanksgiving

One of them, when he saw he was healed, came back, praising God in a loud voice. He threw himself at Jesus' feet and thanked Him.

LUKE 17:15-16

Thanksgiving is verbal, positive and active. It is the giving out of something to God. Thanksgiving is done in the open. Gratitude is secret, silent, passive, not showing its being until expressed in praise and thanksgiving.

Gratitude is felt in the heart. Thanksgiving is the expression of that inward feeling. Thanksgiving is just what the word itself signifies—the giving of thanks to God. It is giving something to God in words that we feel in our heart for blessings received.

DEAR FATHER, I am grateful to You for so many blessings received from Your hand. My heart is filled with gratitude toward You. I praise Your name. Amen.

64

A Fiery Church

Never be lacking in zeal, but keep your spiritual fervor.

ROMANS 12:11

God Himself is all fire; and His church, if it is to be like Him, must also be like white heat. God expects to be represented by a fiery church. The only things that His church can afford to be on fire about are the great, eternal interests of God-given faith.

Our Lord was the incarnate opposite of intolerant and noisy speech. Yet the zeal of God's house consumed Him. And the world is still feeling the glow of His consuming flame. They are responding to it with an ever-increasing readiness and an even larger response.

GOD, I want to be part of a church on fire for You. Help me to never be lacking in zeal but glowing with passion for You. Amen.

65

Zest for Life

"You are neither cold nor hot. I wish you were either one or the other! So, because you are lukewarm—neither hot nor cold—I am about to spit you out of My mouth."

REVELATION 3:15-16

Two things are intolerable to God—insincerity and lukewarmness. Lack of heart and heat are two things God hates. He said that to the Laodiceans.

True prayer must be aflame. The Christian life and character need to be on fire. If man is not wholly interested in the things of heaven, he is not interested in them at all. The fiery souls are those who conquer in the day of battle.

The stronghold of God is taken only by those who storm it in worshipful earnestness and besiege it with fiery, unshaken zeal.

LORD, I know that You hate lukewarmness. I want to be wholly interested in the things of heaven. Please help and guide me through Your Holy Spirit. Amen.

66

Passion for Christ

"Zeal for Thy house will consume me."

JOHN 2:17 RSV

Love is kindled in a flame, and zeal is its fuel. Flame is the air that true Christian experience breathes. It feeds on fire. It can withstand anything except a weak flame.

A lack of passion in prayer is a sure sign of the lack of depth and intensity of desire. To reduce fervor is to retire from God. He can and will pardon sin when the repentant one prays. Fire is the motivating power in prayer.

Religious principles that do not come out of fire have neither force nor effect. Passion is the soul of prayer.

DEAR GOD, I don't want to be lacking in spiritual fervor. Ignite the flames of passion in my soul so that I may serve You wholeheartedly. Amen.

No Prayer without Flame

May my prayer be set before You like incense; may the lifting up of my hands be like the evening sacrifice.

PSALM 141:2

The early Methodists had no heating in their churches. They said that the flame in the pew and the fire in the pulpit must be sufficient to keep them warm. And we, today, need to have the live coal from God's altar in our hearts.

This flame is not mental power or fleshly energy. It is the very being of the Spirit of God. Prayer ascends by fire. Flame gives prayer access as well as wings. It gives prayer acceptance as well as energy. There is no incense without fire, no prayer without flame.

FATHER GOD, I want the burning coal from Your altar in my heart. I pray, Lord, for You to ignite my heart through the power of Your Spirit. Amen.

68

Babbling or Prayer?

My soul thirsts for God, for the living God.

PSALM 42:2

Prayer is not the rehearsal of a mere performance. It is not an indefinite, widespread demand. Prayer is a necessary phase of spiritual habit, but it ceases to be prayer when it is done by habit alone.

It is the depth and strength of spiritual desire that gives intensity to prayer. Many things may be listed and much ground covered. Does desire map out the region to be covered? The answer depends on whether our petitioning is babbling or prayer.

The urgency of our desire holds us to the thing desired with sustained courage. It stays, pleads, persists and refuses to let go until the blessing has been given.

LORD, please guide me so that my prayers will never be mere babbling, but earnest, heartfelt prayer. Amen.

Basis of Prayer

"Blessed are those who hunger and thirst for righteousness, for they will be filled."

MATTHEW 5:6

Desire shoots at its objective. There may be many things that are desired, but they are specifically and individually felt and expressed. It is this singleness of desire, this definite yearning, that counts in prayer and drives it directly to the center of supply.

This is the basis of prayer that expects an answer. It is that strong, inward desire that has entered the spiritual appetite and demands to be satisfied. For us, it is entirely true and frequent that our prayers operate in the dry area of a mere wish or in the lifeless area of a memorized prayer.

Pray fervently and with a sincere yearning for the Lord, and He will draw near to you and satisfy your needs.

DEAR GOD, thank You that we may know that those who hunger and thirst for You, will be satisfied. Amen.

70

A New Discovery

"I will not let you go, unless you bless me."

GENESIS 32:26

Sometimes our prayers are merely stereotyped expressions of set phrases. The freshness and life has gone out long ago.

Without desire, there is no burden of the soul, no vision, and no glow of faith. There is no strong pressure, no holding on to God with a despairing grasp. God draws very close to the praying soul. To see God, know God, and live for God—these form the objective of all true prayer.

So, to those who pray like this, the Bible becomes a new discovery, and Christ a new Savior by the light and revelation gained through your prayers.

DEAR FATHER, through prayer we can discover and experience You anew each day. Thank You for drawing close to the praying soul. Amen.

71

Discerning our Desires

One thing I ask from the Lord, this only do I seek: that I may dwell in the house of the Lord all the days of my life, to gaze on the beauty of the Lord and to seek Him in His temple.

PSALM 27:4

Desire is the will in action. It is a strong and conscious longing that is energized in the inner man for some great good. It contains choice, attitude, and fire. Prayer, based on these characteristics, is genuine and specific.

Holy desire is helped on by devout study. Meditation on our spiritual needs and God's ability to satisfy them, helps desire to grow. Serious thought, practiced before praying, increases desire. It makes prayer more insistent and tends to save us from the danger of wandering thoughts.

FATHER GOD, please guide me through Your Holy Spirit as I meditate on Your Word. You are worthy of our praise. Amen.

Closely Related

Devote yourselves to prayer, being watchful and thankful.

COLOSSIANS 4:2

Prayer, praise and thanksgiving all go together. A close relationship exists among them. The Scriptures join these three things together.

Psalms is filled with many songs of praise and hymns of thanksgiving, all pointing back to the results of prayer. Thanksgiving includes gratitude. In fact, thanksgiving is the expression of an inward, conscious gratitude to God for mercies received.

Gratitude is an inward emotion of the soul, involuntarily arising therein, while thanksgiving is the voluntary expression of gratitude.

DEAR FATHER GOD, I want to give thanks to You with a grateful heart because You have been good to me. Your love endures forever. Amen.

73

GRATITUDE

The LORD *has done great things for us; we are glad.*
PSALM 126:3 RSV

Gratitude arises from a contemplation of the goodness of God. It arises when we meditate on what God has done for us. Gratitude and thanksgiving both point to, and have to do with God and His mercies. The heart is consciously grateful to God. The soul gives expression to that heartfelt gratitude to God in words or acts.

Gratitude is born of meditation on God's grace and mercy. Praise is brought about by gratitude and a conscious obligation to God for mercies given. As we think of mercies past, our hearts are inwardly moved to gratitude.

DEAR GOD, my heart is filled with gratitude toward You for all the grace and mercy You have for Your children. Amen.

74

PRAY FOR DESIRE

What is more, I consider everything a loss because of the surpassing worth of knowing Christ Jesus my Lord, for whose sake I have lost all things. I consider them garbage, that I may gain Christ.

PHILIPPIANS 3:8

Our judgment tells us that we ought to pray, even if we discover that desire is absent. In such circumstances, we ought to pray for the desire to pray. This desire is God-given and heaven-born. When desire has been given, we should pray according to its principles.

The lack of spiritual desire should grieve us and lead us to mourn its absence. We should earnestly seek for its prize so that our praying can be an expression of the soul's sincere desire.

ALMIGHTY GOD, I pray that You will increase and inspire my desire to pray. I want my prayers to be powerful and effective. Amen.

75

Prayer Looks to the Future

Rejoice always, pray continually, give thanks in all circumstances; for this is God's will for you in Christ Jesus.

1 THESSALONIANS 5:16-18

Gratitude and thanksgiving always look at the past, although they also take in the present. But prayer looks to the future. Thanksgiving deals with things already received. Prayer deals with things desired, asked for, and expected.

Prayer turns to gratitude and praise when the things asked for have been granted by God. As prayer brings things to us that produce gratitude and thanksgiving, so praise and gratitude promote prayer and encourage better praying.

FATHER, Your will for us is to pray continually and give thanks in all circumstances. Please help me do this through Your Holy Spirit. Amen.

76

Gratitude and Murmuring

And be thankful...as you teach and admonish one another with all wisdom...singing to God with gratitude in your hearts.

COLOSSIANS 3:15-16

Gratitude and thanksgiving to God stand opposed to our murmuring and complaints about our situation. Gratitude and murmuring never abide in the same heart at the same time. An unappreciative spirit has no standing beside gratitude and praise.

True prayer banishes complaining and promotes gratitude and thanksgiving. Dissatisfaction at one's lot, and a disposition to be discontented with things that come to us in the providence of God, are foes to gratitude and thanksgiving.

LORD, I don't want dissatisfaction to stand in the way of being grateful and giving thanks to You. Please grant me an appreciative and content spirit. Amen.

77

A Consecrated Life = Prayer + Thanksgiving

With thanksgiving, present your requests to God.
PHILIPPIANS 4:6

Wherever there is true prayer, thanksgiving and gratitude are ready to respond to its fulfillment when it comes. As prayer brings the answer, so the answer brings forth gratitude and praise. As prayer sets God to work, so answered prayer sets thanksgiving to work. Thanksgiving follows answered prayer just as day succeeds night.

True prayer and gratitude lead to full consecration, and consecration leads to better praying. A consecrated life is a life of both prayer and thanksgiving.

DEAR GOD, I want to live a consecrated life of prayer and thanksgiving before You. Guide me through the power of Your Spirit. Amen.

78

Sing Praises!

"He who brings thanksgiving as his sacrifice honors Me; to him who orders his way aright I will show the salvation of God!"

PSALM 50:23 RSV

Praise is definitely committed to prayer. Praise is dependent on prayer for its full volume and its sweet melody. Singing is the usual method of praise. The singing service in our churches is important, for according to the character of our singing, the genuineness of our praises will be measured. The singing may be directed in such a way as to have in it elements that deprave and debauch prayer. It may be so directed as to drive away things like thanksgiving and praise.

Most of the singing in our churches today is entirely foreign to hearty, sincere praise to God. Praise God with your sincere songs of joy today and every day.

LORD, I want to sing songs of praise and joy to You. Please help me so that my singing to You may be sincere. Amen.

79

The Fragrance of Prayer

Through Jesus, therefore, let us continually offer to God a sacrifice of praise—the fruit of lips that openly profess His name.

HEBREWS 13:15

The spirit of prayer and of true praise go hand in hand. Both are often entirely driven away by the thoughtless singing in our congregations. A lot of the singing lacks serious thought and is devoid of a devotional spirit.

Giving thanks is the very life of prayer. It is its fragrance and music, its poetry and its crown. Prayer, bringing the desired answer, breaks out into praise and thanksgiving.

Whatever interferes with and injures the spirit of prayer necessarily hurts and dissipates the spirit of praise.

FATHER GOD, my offer to You is my sacrifice of praise. I want to sing of Your love and goodness forever. Amen.

Spiritual Singing

Let everything that has breath praise the Lord. Praise the Lord.

PSALM 150:6

The heart must have in it the grace of prayer to sing the praises of God. Spiritual singing is not done by musical taste or talent, but by the grace of God in your heart. Nothing helps praise so mightily as a gracious revival of true religion in the church.

The conscious presence of God inspires song. The angels and the glorified ones in heaven do not need choirs to chime in with their heavenly praise and worship.

They are not dependent on singing schools to teach them the notes and scale of singing. Their singing involuntarily breaks forth from the heart.

LORD GOD, thank You for inspiring our songs and prayers through Your presence. Amen.

81

God's Presence Results in Singing

How good it is to sing praises to our God, how pleasant and fitting to praise Him!

PSALM 147:1

God is always present in the heavenly assemblies of the angels. His glorious presence creates the song, teaches the singing, and infuses the notes of praise.

The presence of God results in singing and thanksgiving, while the absence of God from our congregations is the death of song, and makes the singing lifeless, cold, and formal.

God's conscious presence in our churches would bring back the days of praise and would restore the full chorus of song.

LORD, together with the psalmist I say, "How good it is to sing praises to our God, how pleasant and fitting to praise Him." Amen.

82

A Spiritual Desire

Like newborn babies, crave pure spiritual milk, so that by it you may grow up.

1 PETER 2:2

A sense of need creates earnest desire. Hunger is an active sense of physical need. It prompts the request for food. In the same way, the inward awareness of spiritual need creates desire, and desire creates prayer.

Desire is a longing in our hearts for something that we do not have. Spiritual desire is the evidence of new life in Christ.

It is born in the renewed soul: The absence of this holy desire in the heart is proof that there has been a decline in spiritual joy or that the new birth has never taken place.

GOD, I pray that my spiritual joy would not decline. I pray for my soul to be renewed by You every day for Your glory. Amen.

83

Specific Prayers

Is anyone among you in trouble? Let them pray. Is anyone happy? Let them sing songs of praise.

James 5:13

God does so much for us, but to get all the things we need, we need to pray a certain kind of prayer. We need to be specific and particular and bring to God, through prayer and thanksgiving, our particular requests; the things we greatly desire. And with it all, accompanying all these requests, there must be thanksgiving.

It is wonderful to know that what God wants us to do on earth, we will be engaged in doing for eternity.

Praise and thanksgiving will be our blessed employment while we remain in heaven. Nor will we ever grow weary of this pleasing task.

GOD ALMIGHTY, I present my requests to You by prayer and petition, with thanksgiving. Thank You for hearing my prayers. Amen.

84

A Praising Spirit

Praise awaits You, our God, in Zion; to You our vows will be fulfilled.

PSALM 65:1

The spirit of praise was once the boast of the early church. This spirit rested on the tabernacles of the early Christians, as a cloud of glory out of which God shone and spoke.

It filled their temples with the perfume of costly, flaming incense. That this spirit of praise is sadly deficient in our present-day congregations must be evident to every careful observer. That it is a mighty force in projecting the gospel, must be equally evident.

To restore the spirit of praise to our congregations should be one of the main objectives of every Christian.

LORD, I want the spirit of praise to return to our congregations so that Your name will be glorified over all the earth. Amen.

85

WAITING FOR THE SPIRIT

All of them were filled with the Holy Spirit.

ACTS 2:4

The promise of the Holy Spirit to the disciples was realized only after many days of persistent prayer.

The promise was clear and definite that the disciples should be gifted with power from on high; they had to stay in Jerusalem.

The fulfillment of the promise depended on the waiting. And it is significant that it was while they were praying, resting their expectations on the surety of the promise, that the Holy Spirit fell upon them and they were all filled. The promise and the prayer went hand in hand.

LORD, thank You that You fill us with Your Holy Spirit if we rest our expectations on Your promises while we pray and wait on You. Amen.

86

THE FAMOUS DAY OF PENTECOST

On one occasion, while He was eating with them, He gave them this command: "Do not leave Jerusalem, but wait for the gift My Father promised, which you have heard Me speak about."

ACTS 1:4

After Jesus Christ made this promise to His disciples, He ascended to heaven. Yet the promise given by Him of sending the Holy Spirit was not fulfilled only by His enthronement.

The answer is found in the fact that His disciples, with the women, spent several days in that Upper Room, in continued prayer. It was prayer that brought to pass the famous Day of Pentecost. And as it was then, so it can be today.

Prayer can bring a Pentecost today if there is the same kind of praying, for the promise has not lost its power and vitality.

GOD, I know that persistent, heartfelt prayer can achieve great things in this world. Please keep me on my knees. Amen.

87

The Abundant Pardon

"Jesus, Son of David, have mercy on me!"

MARK 10:47 RSV

The promises of God to all kinds of sinners are the same. God's promises are fulfilled when sinners repent and ask God for forgiveness.

The praying sinner receives mercy because his prayer is grounded on the promise that if we confess our sins, God will forgive us and purify us. The remorseful one who seeks after God obtains mercy because there is a definite promise of mercy to all who seek the Lord's face.

Prayer always brings forgiveness to the seeking soul. The abundant pardon is dependent upon the promise made real by God's promise to the sinner.

LORD, thank You for Your promise that if we confess our sins, You are faithful and just and will forgive us our sins and purify us from all unrighteousness. Amen.

88

Hold On, Press On and Wait

Jesus told His disciples a parable to show them that they should always pray and not give up.

LUKE 18:1

The parable that comes after these words was taught with the intention of saving people from faintheartedness in prayer. Our Lord wanted to teach us to guard against negligence, and encourage us to show persistence.

Persistent prayer is a mighty move of the soul toward God. It is the ability to hold on, press on, and wait. Restless desire, restful patience, and strength to hold on are all embraced in it. It is not merely a routine, but a passion of soul. It is not something half-needed, but a sheer necessity.

DEAR FATHER, save me from faint-heartedness when I pray. Teach me persistence and the ability to hold on, press on and wait. Amen.

89

WRESTLING IN PRAYER

The prayer of a righteous person is powerful and effective.

JAMES 5:16

Wrestling in persistent prayer does not mean physical violence or fleshly energy. It is an inward force or ability planted and inspired by the Holy Spirit. In effect, it is the intercession of the Spirit of God in us.

The divine Spirit supplies us with the energy of His own determination. This is the essence of the persistence that urges our praying to continue until the blessings descend.

This wrestling in prayer is not loud, but firm and urgent. When there are no visible outlets for its mighty forces, it may be silent.

DEAR GOD, thank You for Your Holy Spirit who intercedes for us when we wrestle in prayer. Amen.

90

Take Heart

"In this world you will have trouble. But take heart! I have overcome the world."

JOHN 16:33

In the New Testament there are three words used that mean trouble. They are tribulation, suffering and affliction. These words differ somewhat, and yet, each of them means trouble of some kind.

Our Lord told His disciples to expect tribulation in this life, teaching them that tribulation belongs to this world; that they could not hope to escape it, and that they would not be carried through this life on flowery beds of comfort.

This is a hard lesson to learn. We can, however, take heart, because God has overcome the world. Through Him, we are victors.

LORD, I rejoice in Your name. Although we will face troubles of many kinds, we can be sure that You will carry us through them because You have already overcome this world. Amen.

91

CONTINUAL PRAYER

Rejoice always, pray continually, give thanks in all circumstances; for this is God's will for you in Christ Jesus.

1 THESSALONIANS 5:16-18

Nothing distinguishes the children of God so clearly and strongly as prayer. It is the one infallible mark of being a Christian. But even the Christian has to cultivate continual prayer. It must be habitual, but it must be much more than just a habit.

It is a duty, one that rises far above the ordinary implications of the term. It is the expression of a relationship with God, a yearning for divine communion.

It is the flow of the soul toward its original fountain. It is a statement of the soul's origin, a claiming of sonship that links man to the eternal.

ALMIGHTY GOD, I want to be distinguished as Your child through my prayers to You. My soul yearns to come into Your presence every day. Amen.

92

The Horizon of Hope

"These are they who have come out of the great tribulation; they have washed their robes and made them white in the blood of the Lamb. And God will wipe away every tear from their eyes."

REVELATION 7:14, 17

Trouble makes the earth undesirable and creates a desire for heaven within us. There where trouble never comes. It is the path of tribulation that leads to that world.

Hear John as he talked about it and those who will be there. Children of God, you who have suffered, who have been greatly tried, whose sad experiences have often produced broken spirits and bleeding hearts, cheer up!

God is in all your troubles, you just have to be patient, submissive and consistent in prayer.

FATHER GOD, in this world I've experienced suffering. Please help me to be patient, submissive and prayerful, for You are in all my troubles. Thank You, Lord. Amen.

93

MOSES, ELIJAH AND JESUS

Then Jesus told His disciples a parable to show them that they should always pray and not give up.

LUKE 18:1

Moses prayed for forty days to stop the wrath of God. His example is an encouragement to present-day faith in its darkest hour.

Elijah repeated his prayer seven times before the rain clouds appeared on the horizon.

During His earthly life, the blessed Savior spent many nights in prayer. In Gethsemane He presented the same petition three times with unshaken, yet submissive persistence. This called on every part of His soul and brought about tears and bloody sweat.

Jesus' life victories were all won in hours of persistent prayer. He taught, by example, the importance of consistent prayer.

DEAR FATHER, thank You for Jesus' example of praying day and night and not giving up. Amen.

94

God Rewards Abundantly

And the Lord said, "Listen to what the unjust judge says. And will not God bring about justice for His chosen ones, who cry out to Him day and night?"

LUKE 18:6-7

He who does not push his plea does not pray at all. Prayers with no heart have no claim on heaven and no hearing in the courts above. God waits patiently as His people cry to Him day and night. He is moved by their requests a thousand times more than this unjust judge was.

Waiting for answers to prayer is limited by persistent praying, and the answer is richly given. God sees His praying child's faith. He honors this faith that stays and cries by persisting in prayer, so that it is strengthened and enriched. Then He rewards it abundantly.

LORD, thank You for richly rewarding persistent praying. Thank You for seeing my faith when I pray. Amen.

95

SUCCESSFUL PERSISTENCE

"Lord, help me!"

MATTHEW 15:25 RSV

The Canaanite woman, who came to Jesus on behalf of her daughter, is a notable instance of successful persistence. It is one that is highly encouraging to all who pray successfully. Her heart was in her prayer.

At first, Jesus appears to pay no attention to her agony and ignores her cry for relief. She came closer, cutting her prayer in half, and fell at His feet. Worshiping Him, she made her daughter's case known.

This last cry won her case. Her daughter was healed that same hour.

Hopeful, urgent, and unwearied, she stayed near the Master, insisting and praying until the answer was given. What an example of persistence!

ALMIGHTY GOD, I want to pray persistently, like the Canaanite woman. In worship I make my case known to You. Amen.

96

Clinging Faith

"Woman, you have great faith! Your request is granted."

MATTHEW 15:28

The Canaanite woman gives a glimpse of her clinging faith, and her spiritual insight. The Master went to the Sidonian country so that this truth could be shown for all time: There is no cry as effective as persistent prayer, and there is no prayer to which God surrenders Himself so fully and so freely.

The persistence of this distressed mother brought about her request. Instead of being an offense to the Savior, it drew from Him a word of wonder and glad surprise.

DEAR LORD GOD, please increase my faith and help me to pray persistently. Amen.

97

SUFFERINGS

I consider that our present sufferings are not worth comparing with the glory that will be revealed in us.
ROMANS 8:18

Paul used the word *sufferings* to describe the troubles of life in the comforting passage where he contrasted life's troubles to the final glory of heaven, which shall be the reward of all who patiently endure until the end.

Further, he spoke of the afflictions that come to the people of God in this world, and he regarded them as nearly weightless when compared to the weight of glory awaiting all who are submissive, patient and faithful in all their troubles.

GOD, make me a patient and faithful servant so that Your glory may be revealed in me. Amen.

AFFLICTIONS

For our light and momentary troubles are achieving for us an eternal glory that far outweighs them all.
2 CORINTHIANS 4:17

Our afflictions can work for us only if we co-operate with God in prayer. God can accomplish His highest ends for us through prayer. His providence works best when His people pray. They know that trouble serves a purpose. They know that God can use trouble to strengthen their relationship with Him.

The greatest value in trouble comes to those who turn to God in prayer. In fact, the only way to endure trouble patiently, is to pray consistently.

The school of prayer is where patience is learned and practiced.

ALMIGHTY GOD, I want to learn from my troubles. I bow before You in prayer. Amen.

99

A Chain of Graces

We also glory in our sufferings, because we know that suffering produces perseverance; perseverance, character; and character, hope. And hope does not put us to shame, because God's love has been poured out into our hearts through the Holy Spirit, who has been given to us.

ROMANS 5:3-5

Prayer brings us into that state of grace where suffering cannot only be endured, but where there is a spirit of rejoicing over it. What a chain of graces that could flow from tribulation.

It is in the furnace that faith is tested, patience is tried, and where all those rich virtues are developed that make up Christian character.

It is while they are passing through deep waters that God shows how close He can come to His praying, believing saints.

FATHER, thank You for drawing close to us when we need You most. When we go through deep waters, Your presence comes very close to us. Amen.

100

MOLDING THE SOUL

Therefore we do not lose heart. Though outwardly we are wasting away, yet inwardly we are being renewed day by day.

2 CORINTHIANS 4:16

Prayer has everything to do with molding the soul into the image of God. It has everything to do with enriching, broadening, and maturing the soul's experience of God.

A man who does not pray cannot possibly be called a Christian.

Prayer is the only way the soul can enter into fellowship and communion with the Source of all Christlike spirit and energy. Therefore, if he does not pray, he is not of the household of faith.

DEAR GOD, I thank You that I can enter into fellowship and communion with You through my prayers. Amen.

101

An All-Wise Designer

Be joyful in hope, patient in affliction, faithful in prayer.

ROMANS 12:12

God's highest aim in dealing with His people is to develop a Christian character in them. He is seeking to make us like Himself. God wants to create in us a spirit of patience, meekness, and submission to His will. He wants us to carry everything to Him in prayer.

And trouble in any form tends to do this very thing, for this is the end and aim of trouble. This is its work.

It is not a chance incident in life, but has a design in view, just as it has an all-wise Designer. God uses trouble to draw us closer to Him.

O LORD, I know that You shape my character through suffering. Please help me to be joyful always, and patient in affliction. Amen.

102

Trouble Attracts Attention

"When he came to his senses, he said, 'How many of my father's hired servants have food to spare, and here I am starving to death!'"

LUKE 15:17

Just as prayer is wide in its range, so trouble is infinitely varied in its uses. Trouble is sometimes used to attract attention and to stop people in the busy rush of life.

The prodigal son was independent and self-sufficient when it went well with him. But, when money and friends departed, he decided to return to his father's house. Through trouble many a man who has forgotten God has been stopped, caused to consider his ways, and brought to remember God and pray. Blessed is trouble when it accomplishes this in people's lives!

DEAR GOD, use my troubles to let me consider my ways, bring me back to praying and fix my eyes on You. Amen.

103

The Possibilities of Prayer

Open wide your mouth and I will fill it.

PSALM 81:10

How vast are the possibilities of prayer! It lays its hand on God Almighty and moves Him to do what He would not otherwise do if prayer were not offered.

Prayer is a wonderful power placed by God in the hands of His people, which may be used to accomplish great purposes and to achieve unusual results. Prayer reaches to everything, taking in all things great and small that are promised by God to His children.

O FATHER, I thank You for the wonderful power of prayer that You placed in our hands. Amen.

104

PRAYER PROVES ITSELF

"Anyone who chooses to do the will of God will find out whether My teaching comes from God."

JOHN 7:17

The records of the achievements of prayer are encouraging to faith.

Prayer is no untried theory. Prayer is a divine arrangement from God; designed for the benefit of mankind, intended as a means for furthering the interests of His cause on earth, and carrying out His gracious purposes in redemption and providence. Prayer proves itself. It is capable of proving its virtue through those who pray. Prayer needs no proof other than its accomplishments.

If any man wants to know the virtue of prayer, if he wants to know what it can achieve, let him pray. Let him put prayer to the test.

DEAR LORD GOD, thank You that prayer is no untried theory. It is a divine arrangement from You for our benefit, and for carrying out Your plans on earth for Your glory. Amen.

105

A Soul Set Alight for God

And pray for us, too, that God may open a door for our message.

COLOSSIANS 4:3

How vast are the possibilities of prayer! What great things are accomplished by this divinely appointed means of grace! It is the breathing of a soul inflamed for God and inflamed for man.

Prayer opens possibilities for the spread of the gospel. Prayer moves God to do His work in new and enlarged ways. Prayer not only gives great power, it also helps you to spread the gospel.

Prayer makes the gospel move with glorious speed. It moves with God's power and with saintly swiftness.

GOD, I know that through prayer I can open doors for the mighty work of Your Spirit to spread the Good News. Please help me to never grow weary in prayer. Amen.

106

GO GOSPEL GO!

Brothers and sisters, pray for us that the message of the Lord may spread rapidly and be honored.

2 THESSALONIANS 3:1

The gospel moves altogether too slowly, often timidly, and with feeble steps. What will make this gospel move rapidly, like an athlete in a race? The answer is at hand.

Prayer, more prayer and better prayer will do the deed. This means of grace will give swiftness, splendor, and divinity to the gospel. The possibilities of prayer reach to all things.

Whatever concerns man's welfare and whatever has to do with God's plans and purposes concerning people on earth can be a subject for prayer.

DEAR FATHER GOD, I want to help move Your message faster to all people. Guide me through Your Spirit to pray always and about all things. Amen.

107

WHATEVER

"I will do whatever you ask in My name, so that the Father may be glorified in the Son. You may ask Me for anything in My name, and I will do it."

JOHN 14:13-14

"Whatever you ask" embraces all that concerns God's praying people. And whatever is left out of "whatever" is left out of prayer. Where will we draw the lines that will leave out or limit the word "whatever"?

Define it, and search out and publish the things that the word does not include. If "whatever" does not include all things, then substitute the word with "anything". The possibilities of prayer are unspeakable, but who has learned the lesson of prayer; who realizes and measures up to these possibilities?

DEAR GOD, thank You that we can pray to You about anything. Amen.

108

Increased Praying

"Very truly I tell you, My Father will give you whatever you ask in My name."

JOHN 16:23

Here is a very definite catchphrase from our Lord to increase our praying. We are definitely urged by Him to ask for large things, and the dignity and solemnity of this announcement is indicated by the phrase, "I tell you the truth."

Why are these words recorded in this last and vital conversation of our Lord with His disciples?

The answer is that our Lord wanted to prepare them for the new dispensation in which prayer was to have marvelous results and be the chief agency to conserve and make His gospel flourish.

FATHER GOD, I want my prayers to You to make the gospel flourish. Please guide me when I pray so that Your name may be glorified. Amen.

109

The Fruit of Prayer

"You did not choose me, but I chose you and appointed you so that you might go and bear fruit—fruit that will last—and so that whatever you ask in My name the Father will give you."

JOHN 15:16

In our Lord's generous statement to His disciples about choosing them so that they would bear fruit, He clearly teaches that this matter of praying and fruit bearing is not a petty business of our choice.

He specifically had our praying in mind; He has chosen us of His own divine selection; and He expects us to do this one thing of praying, and to do it well.

The main objective of choosing us as His disciples and of sharing friendship with Him was that we might be better fitted to bear the fruit of prayer.

O GOD, You have chosen me of Your own divine selection. I want to do what You require from us—to pray, and to do it well. Amen.

110

God Answers Prayer

"Everything is possible for one who believes."

MARK 9:23

We affirm with absolute certainty that God answers prayer. He hears and answers every prayer where the true conditions of praying are met. This is either true or not. If not, then there is nothing in prayer. Then prayer becomes but the recitation of words.

But if what the Scripture verse says is true, then there are vast possibilities in prayer. Then it is far-reaching in its scope and wide in its range.

Then it is true that prayer can lay its hand upon God Almighty and move Him to do great and wonderful things.

ALMIGHTY FATHER, I believe that everything is possible for those who believe in You. Thank You that our prayers can move You to do great things. Amen.

111

God Means What He Says

The hope of eternal life, which God, who does not lie, promised before the beginning of time.

TITUS 1:2

Let us always keep in mind and never for one moment allow ourselves to doubt the statement that God means what He says in all His promises. God's promises are His own Word.

But we have failed to express ourselves fully in prayer. The ability to pray can be secured by the grace and power of the Holy Spirit, but it demands such a strenuous and noble character that it is a rare thing for a man or woman to be on praying ground and on pleading terms with God.

DEAR GOD, through the grace, mercy and power of Your Holy Spirit our ability to pray can be secured. I thank You, Lord. Amen.

THE TWINS: PRAYER AND FAITH

"For He who promised is faithful."

HEBREWS 10:23

The possibilities of prayer are the possibilities of faith. Prayer and faith are Siamese twins. One heart brings them both to life. Faith is always praying; prayer is always believing. Faith must have a tongue by which it can speak; prayer is the tongue of faith. Faith must receive; prayer is the hand of faith stretched out to receive.

Prayer must rise and soar; faith must give prayer the wings to fly and ascend. Prayer must have an audience with God; faith opens the door and an audience is given. Prayer asks; faith lays its hand on the thing asked for.

FATHER GOD, through my faith in You I am moved to pray, and through my prayers I believe that You can do immeasurably more than we can ask or imagine. Amen.

113

THE SUM OF RELIGION

"Nothing will be impossible for you."

MATTHEW 17:20 RSV

Prayer is not an indifferent, small thing. It is not a sweet little privilege. It is a great prerogative, far-reaching in its effects. Failure to pray entails great loss. Prayer is not just an episode of the Christian life.

Life is a preparation for and the result of prayer. In its condition, prayer is the sum of religion.

Prayer is not only the language of spiritual life, but prayer also makes its very essence and forms its innermost, real character.

GOD, thank You for granting us the great privilege of prayer that has far-reaching effects. Amen.

114

THE GIFT OF ANOINTMENT

For it is by grace you have been saved, through faith—and this is not from yourselves, it is the gift of God.

EPHESIANS 2:8

It is an anointed preacher who stirs many congregations.

It belongs to the experience of the man as well as to his preaching. It is that which transforms him into the image of his divine Master, as well as that by which he declares the truths of Christ with power.

This anointing is not a fixed gift. It is a conditional gift. This anointing comes directly from God in answer to prayer. Prayer, much prayer, is the price of anointment.

Without perseverance in prayer, the anointing, like over-kept manna, breeds worms.

DEAR FATHER, I want to receive Your gift of anointing. I know that this anointing comes directly from You in answer to prayer. Please help me persevere in prayer. Amen.

115

THE DIVINE COMFORTER

The Spirit intercedes for God's people in accordance with the will of God.

ROMANS 8:27

The Comforter plants Himself not in the mountain, but in the middle of the human heart, to rouse it to the struggle and to teach it the need of prayer.

The Divine Comforter puts the burden of earth's need into human hearts and makes human lips give voice to their unutterable groaning!

What a mighty Christ of prayer is the Holy Spirit! How He quenches every flame in the heart but the flame of heavenly desire! How He quiets, like a weaned child, all the self-will, until we pray only as He prays.

O FATHER, I thank You that Your Spirit intercedes for us in accordance to Your will. What a mighty God we serve. Amen.

116

PREACHING BY EXAMPLE

Like newborn babies, crave pure spiritual milk, so that by it you may grow up in your salvation.

1 PETER 2:2

The work of God in the world is the perfection of holiness in His people. Keep this in mind. But we might ask: Is this work advancing in the church?

The present-day church owns the latest technological equipment. But the church must, however, not lose sight of its most important purpose, namely to lead people to live holy lives through prayer. Ministers, like laymen, must be holy in life, in conversation and in temper.

They must be examples to the flock of God in all things. By their lives they are to preach as well as reflect the image of our Lord.

O FATHER, I want to reflect Your image to the world. Please guide me through the help of Your precious Holy Spirit. Amen.

Pray and Be Prayed For

I urge you, brothers and sisters, by our Lord Jesus Christ and by the love of the Spirit, to join me in my struggle by praying to God for me.

ROMANS 15:30

For the preacher, prayer is not simply the duty of his profession, but a privilege. It is a necessity. Air is not more necessary to the lungs than prayer is to the preacher. The preacher must pray; the preacher must be prayed for. These two propositions are wedded into a union that should never be separated.

It will take all the praying he can do, to meet the fearful responsibilities and success in his great work. The true preacher realizes the importance of prayer and spiritual growth. He therefore values it when God's people pray for him.

DEAR GOD, I pray for our pastor today. Help and guide him in his important work and bless him with Your abundant blessings. Amen.

118

Prayerless Christians

Pray for us, too, that God may open a door for our message, so that we may proclaim the mystery of Christ, for which I am in chains. Pray that I may proclaim it clearly, as I should.

COLOSSIANS 4:3-4

The more holy a person is, the more he values prayer; the clearer he sees that God gives Himself to praying people. The Holy Spirit never abides in a spirit that does not pray. Christ knows nothing of prayerless Christians.

Gifts, talents, education, eloquence, and God's call cannot lessen the demand of prayer, but only intensify the necessity for the preacher to pray and to be prayed for. And, if he is a true preacher, he will feel the necessity of prayer even more strongly.

He will not only feel the increasing demand to pray himself, but to call on others to help him through their prayers.

FATHER, I pray for preachers; that You will open the doors for their message as they tell the world of Your love for us. Amen.

119

The Church Equals Its Leaders

Stand firm in all the will of God, mature and fully assured.

COLOSSIANS 4:12

Preachers are pre-eminently God's leaders. They are primarily responsible for the condition of the Church. They shape its character and give tone and direction to its life. Much depends on these leaders. They shape the times and the institutions.

The Church is divine; the treasure it holds is heavenly. But it bears the imprint of the human. The treasure is in earthen vessels. The Church of God makes, or is made by its leaders. The Church will be what its leaders are: spiritual if they are so; worldly if they are; conglomerate if its leaders are.

O GOD, I pray for the leaders in my church today and the important work they do. Bless them, Lord, but lead them also to lead us to be more like You. Amen.

120

A PULPIT WITHOUT PRAYER

Know this love that surpasses knowledge—that you may be filled to the measure of all the fullness of God.

EPHESIANS 3:19

Strong spiritual leaders—people of holy might—are tokens of God's favor. Times of spiritual leadership are times of great spiritual prosperity to the church. Prayer is one of the eminent characteristics of strong spiritual leadership.

People of mighty prayer are people of power, and they shape the outcome of things. How can a person who does not get his message fresh from God in prayer expect to preach? A preacher's lips must be touched by the burning flame of prayer.

As far as the real interests of Christianity are concerned, a pulpit without prayer will always be a barren thing.

ALMIGHTY GOD, fill me and fill our spiritual leaders with the measure of all the fullness of You. Amen.

121

Paul, the Preacher

And pray in the Spirit on all occasions with all kinds of prayers and requests. With this in mind, be alert and always keep on praying for all the Lord's people. Pray also for me, that whenever I speak, words may be given me so that I will fearlessly make known the mystery of the gospel.

EPHESIANS 6:18-19

A preacher may preach in an official, or learned way, without really praying. But there is an immeasurable distance between this kind of preaching and the sowing of God's precious seed with holy hands and prayerful hearts. Paul is an illustration of this. He exemplifies the fact that the preacher must be a man given to prayer. Paul demonstrates that a true preacher must have the prayers of other good people to give to his ministry its full quota of success.

DEAR GOD, I pray for our pastor and all preachers that whenever they open their mouths, You will give them words that will make the mystery of the gospel known. Amen.

Holy Praying

The smoke of the incense, together with the prayers of God's people, went up before God from the angel's hand.

REVELATION 8:4

It is important to understand that the praying that is given such a position as explained in Revelation, and from which great results flow, is not simply the saying of prayers, but holy praying.

Behind such praying, giving to it energy and flame, are men and women who are whole-heartedly devoted to God. They are entirely separated from sin and fully separated to God. They always give energy, force and strength to praying.

Our Lord Jesus Christ excelled in prayer because He was supreme in holiness.

Full surrender opens the door to the throne of grace. It influences God greatly.

DEAR HEAVENLY FATHER, please guide me through Your Spirit so that my prayers will not be mere words uttered, but holy praying. Amen.

Compassion for Others

The Lord *is gracious and compassionate, slow to anger and rich in love.*

PSALM 145:8

Compassion develops and grows when a person is confronted by the deep needs and distress of people who are unable to help themselves. Helplessness appeals to compassion.

Compassion is silent, but does not remain secluded. It reaches out at the sight of trouble, sin and need.

First of all, compassion flows out in earnest prayer for those in need and has sympathy for them. Prayer for others is born of a sympathetic heart. Prayer is natural and almost spontaneous when compassion grows in the heart. Prayer belongs to the compassionate believer.

DEAR GOD, please grant me a compassionate and sympathetic heart for people. I want my prayers for others to flow from a heart overflowing with compassion. Amen.

124

THE SCHOOL OF SUFFERING

"You may ask Me for anything in My name, and I will do it."

JOHN 14:14

Loving obedience moves us into the prayer realm. It makes us co-heirs of the wealth of Christ. We receive the riches of His grace through the Holy Spirit, who will abide with us and be in us. Obedience to God qualifies us to pray effectively. Jesus learned obedience through suffering. At the same time, He learned prayer through obediencc. Just as it is the prayer of a righteous person that avails much, so it is righteousness that is obedient to God.

A righteous person is an obedient person. He can accomplish great things when he goes to his knees in prayer.

ALMIGHTY GOD, I know that the prayer of a righteous man is powerful and effective. But I also know that righteousness means obeying You. Please help me be obedient. I want to glorify You with my life. Amen.

125

Prayer That Waits

Let them give thanks to the Lord *for His unfailing love and His wonderful deeds for mankind, for He satisfies the thirsty and fills the hungry with good things.*

PSALM 107:8-9

There are many great misconceptions of the true elements and functions of prayer. There are many who earnestly desire to obtain an answer to their prayers, but who go unrewarded and unblessed.

They fix their minds on some great promise of God. This fixing of the mind on something great may help in strengthening faith. But persistent and urgent prayer—prayer that waits until faith increases—must be added to this promise.

Who is able and competent to do such praying except the person who readily, cheerfully and continually *obeys* God?

LORD, thank You, that You satisfy and fill us with good things. I fix my eyes on You as I pray for a more obedient heart. Amen.

126

THE FRUIT OF PRAYER IS...FAITH!

"You will keep in perfect peace those whose minds are steadfast, because they trust in You."

ISAIAH 26:3

Faith is the attitude as well as the act of a soul surrendered to God. His Word and His Spirit dwell in that soul.

It is true that faith must exist in some form or another in order to bring forth praying. But in its strongest form and in its greatest results, faith is the fruit of prayer.

It is true that faith increases the ability and efficiency of prayer. It is likewise true that prayer increases the ability and efficiency of faith. Prayer and faith work, act, and react together.

LOVING FATHER, I surrender my soul to You. Guide me in Your truth and lead me in the way everlasting. Amen.

127

Moving Compassion

When He saw the crowds, He had compassion on them, because they were harassed and helpless, like sheep without a Shepherd.

MATTHEW 9:36

First, He saw the crowds with their hunger and helpless condition; then He felt compassion that moved Him to pray for the crowds.

Hard is the person, and far from being Christ-like, who sees the multitudes but is unmoved at the sight of their sad state, their unhappiness, and their distress. He has no heart of prayer for others.

Compassion may not always move people, but it should always move toward others. And where it is most helpless to relieve the needs of others, it can at least pray earnestly to God for other people.

FATHER GOD, I don't want to be unmoved at the sight of crowds desperately needing Your healing touch. Where I can relieve the needs of others, please help me and where I can't, help me pray. Amen.

128

SUPERHUMAN

I can do all this through Him who gives me strength.
PHILIPPIANS 4:13

It is true that obedience to God helps faith as no other attribute possibly can. When a person recognizes the validity and supremacy of God's divine commands, faith in God becomes an easy task. Obedience to God makes it easy to believe and trust God.

Where the spirit of obedience totally saturates the soul, and the will is perfectly surrendered to God, faith becomes a reality. Faith then becomes almost involuntary. After obedience it is the next natural step.

The difficulty in prayer then is not faith, but obedience, which is faith's foundation.

LORD, I want my faith in You to be a living reality. Make me an obedient servant so that Your name may be glorified over all the earth. Amen.

129

TRUST AND OBEY

Those who know Your name trust in You, for You, LORD, have never forsaken those who seek You.

PSALM 9:10

If we want to pray well and get the most out of our praying, we must look at our obedience. This brings us closer to God.

Disobedient living produces extremely poor praying. No man can pray—really pray—who does not obey.

Our will must be surrendered to the Father as a primary condition to all successful praying. Everything about us receives its coloring from our innermost character.

Our will determines our character and controls our conduct. We've "simply got to trust and obey. There's no other way to be happy in Jesus—but to trust and obey!"

HEAVENLY FATHER, I surrender my will to You. You will give joy and happiness if we only obey and trust in You. Amen.

Spiritual Compassion

Even in darkness light dawns for the upright, for those who are gracious and compassionate and righteous.

PSALM 112:4

We are speaking particularly about spiritual compassion here, that which is born in a renewed heart.

This compassion has in it the quality of mercy, is sympathetic, and moves the soul with a feeling of tenderness for others.

Compassion is moved at the sight of sin, sorrow, and suffering. It stands at the other extreme to indifference to the wants and woes of others. It is far removed from insensibility and hardness of heart in the midst of need and trouble.

Compassion stands beside sympathy for others, is interested in them, and is concerned about them.

ALMIGHTY GOD, where I see suffering, sin and sorrow in the world, make me Your hands and feet to help those thirsty for You. Amen.

131

The Will of the Father

Holy, blameless, pure, set apart from sinners.

HEBREWS 7:26

Our Lord Jesus Christ, had ready access to God in prayer. He had this free, full access because of His unquestioning obedience to His Father. Throughout His earthly life His supreme desire was to do the will of His Father. This fact, as well as others—the consciousness of having His life ordered this way—gave Him confidence and assurance.

It enabled Him to draw near to the throne of grace with unlimited confidence born of obedience, promised acceptance, audience and answer.

Loving obedience puts us where we can ask anything in His name. It gives us the assurance that He will do it.

FATHER GOD, I draw near to Your throne in loving obedience and in awe at Your goodness. Thank You for the assurance that if we draw near to You, You will draw near to us. Amen.

132

Compassion of the Soul

"Go in peace; keep warm and well fed."

JAMES 2:16

There is a certain compassion that is inborn to man, that gives simple gifts to those in need.

But spiritual compassion, the kind born in a renewed heart that is Christlike in nature, is deeper, broader, and more prayerlike. The compassion of Christ always moves to prayer.

Compassion is not blind. He who has compassion of the soul has eyes, first of all to see the things that excite compassion. He who has no eyes to see the exceeding sinfulness of sin, the wants and the sorrows of humanity, will never have compassion for humanity.

DEAR FATHER, please open my eyes to the sinfulness and the hurt in this world. I want to make a difference in the lives of people so that Your name may be glorified. Guide me please. Amen.

133

Praying and Doing

"Not everyone who says to Me, 'Lord, Lord,' will enter the kingdom of heaven, but only the one who does the will of my Father who is in heaven."

MATTHEW 7:21

True praying is not mere eloquent speech. It does not consist of saying in sweet tones, "Lord, Lord." *Prayer is obedience.* Only those who obey have the right to pray. Behind the praying must be the doing. It is the constant doing of God's will in daily life that gives prayer its potency.

No name, however precious and powerful, can protect and give efficiency to prayer that is unaccompanied by doing God's will. Neither can the doing, without the praying, protect from divine disapproval. If prayer does not inspire, sanctify, and direct our work, then self-will enters and ruins both the work and the worker.

ALMIGHTY GOD, I pray that through the help of Your indwelling Spirit, my prayers will not merely be sweet tones, but effective words. Amen.

134

Compassion for Sinners

Because of the L*ORD'S great love we are not consumed, for His compassions never fail.*

LAMENTATIONS 3:22

Compassion has not only to do with the body and its needs. The soul's distressing state, its needs, and its dangers, all ask for compassion.

The highest state of grace is known by compassion for sinners.

This sort of compassion belongs to grace and sees not only the bodies of people, but their immortal spirits—soiled by sin, unhappy without God, and in peril of being lost forever.

When compassion sees dying people hurrying to God, then it breaks out into intercessions for these sinful people.

FATHER GOD, I praise You for Your mercy and compassion. Thank You for the knowledge that Your compassion, mercy and love never fails! Amen.

135

God Is Sovereign

"For My thoughts are not your thoughts, neither are your ways My ways," declares the LORD.

ISAIAH 55:8

God is the Sovereign of earth, of heaven, and of the choice of laborers in His harvest. He delegates to no one else.

Prayer honors God as sovereign and moves Him to His wise and holy selection. Prayer gets God to send forth the best candidates and the most fit people and the people best qualified to work in the harvest.

Compassion for the world of sinners redeemed by Christ, will move the church to pray for them and stir the church to pray to the Lord of the harvest to send forth laborers into the harvest field.

FATHER GOD, I know that You don't always use the most qualified person to do Your work. Sometimes You use ordinary people like me, and equip them to work in Your harvest. Amen.

136

THE GREAT HIGH PRIEST

For we do not have a high priest who is unable to empathize with our weaknesses, but we have one who has been tempted in every way, just as we are—yet he did not sin.

HEBREWS 4:15

What great comfort can fill our hearts when we think of One in heaven who lives to intercede for us. The Lord is compassionate and gracious. He is our Great High Priest.

Moreover, if He is filled with such compassion that it moves Him at the Father's right hand to intercede for us, then in everything we should have the same compassion on others and pray for them regularly.

Just as far as we are compassionate will we be able to pray for others.

LORD JESUS, I want to thank You for interceding for us with the Father. Grant me some of Your compassion for the people around me who are in need. Amen.

137

A Sacred Place

May God Himself, the God of peace, sanctify you through and through. May your whole spirit, soul and body be kept blameless at the coming of our Lord Jesus Christ.

1 THESSALONIANS 5:23

Prayer affects places, times, occasions, and circumstances. It has to do with God and with everything that is related to God.

Prayer has an intimate and special relationship to God's house. A church should be a sacred place, set apart from all unholy and secular uses, for the worship of God. As worship is prayer, the house of God is a place set apart for worship.

It is no common place. It is where God dwells, where He meets with His people, and where He delights in the worship of His saints.

ALMIGHTY GOD, thank You that we can meet with fellow believers at church to worship You and be in Your presence. Help us to keep Your house a sacred place of worship and praise. Amen.

138

Perfectly at Home

"It is written," He said to them, "My house will be called a house of prayer."

MATTHEW 21:13

Prayer is always welcome in the house of God. When prayer is a stranger there, it stops to be God's house.

Our Lord put particular emphasis on what the church should be when He cast out the buyers and sellers in the temple. He makes prayer the most important thing above all else in the house of God. Those who sidetrack prayer misrepresent the church of God and make it into something less than it is meant to be.

Prayer is perfectly at home in the house of God. It is no stranger or guest; it belongs there. It has a divine appointment to be there.

FATHER GOD, hear our prayers as they go up to You when we meet together in church to glorify You. Amen.

139

THE MISSIONARY SPIRIT

May people ever pray for Him.

PSALM 72:15

Psalm 72 is prophetic as it deals with the Messiah. Prayer would be made for His coming to save man, and prayer would be made for the success of the plan of salvation that Jesus would come to set in motion.

The Spirit of Jesus Christ is the spirit of missions. Our Lord Jesus Christ Himself was the first missionary. His promise and arrival put the first missionary movement in action. The missionary spirit is not simply a phase of the gospel, not just a feature of the plan of salvation, but is its very spirit and life. Whoever is touched by the Spirit of God is inspired to spread the Good News all over the world.

HOLY GOD, touch me with Your Spirit, so that others may see more of Jesus in me. Amen.

140

Fears of Tomorrow

"Therefore do not worry about tomorrow."

MATTHEW 6:34

The word *worry* implies to be drawn in all different directions, distracted, anxious, disturbed, upset in spirit. Jesus had warned against this very thing in the Sermon on the Mount.

He was trying to show His people the true secret of a quiet mind, freed from anxiety and unnecessary worry about food and clothing. Tomorrow's evils were not to be considered.

In warning against the fears of tomorrow, evils and the material wants of the body, our Lord was teaching the great lesson of complete and childlike confidence in God.

DEAR LORD, thank You for the great lessons we can learn by reading Your Word. Thank You for knowing our every need, and satisfying them all. Amen.

141

The Holy Place

These things I remember, as I pour out my soul: how I went with the throng, and led them in procession to the house of God, with glad shouts and songs of thanksgiving, a multitude keeping festival.

PSALM 42:4 RSV

Prayer converts the bricks, cement and wood into a sanctuary, a Holy of Holies, where the Lord dwells. Prayer separates the church, in spirit and in purpose, from all other buildings.

With prayer, the house of God becomes a divine sanctuary. So the tabernacle, moving about from place to place, became the Most Holy Place, because God and prayer were there.

Without prayer, the building may be costly, perfect in its structure, attractive to the eye, but it becomes human, with nothing divine in it.

GOD, through our prayers to You, we change a building into a sanctuary of worship. Thank You for the great gift of prayer. Amen.

142

GOD-CALLED MEN

Jesus looked at them and said, "With man this is impossible, but not with God; all things are possible with God."

MARK 10:27

If God's people would pray as they ought to pray, the great things that happened in the past would happen again. The gospel would advance with a facility and power it has never known. If Christians prayed as Christians ought, with strong, commanding faith, with earnestness and sincerity, God-called people, God-empowered people, would be burning to go and spread the gospel worldwide. The God-inspired person would go and kindle the flame of sacred fire for Christ, everywhere in all nations.

Soon all people would hear the glad tidings of salvation and have an opportunity to receive Jesus Christ as their personal Savior.

DEAR FATHER, please guide me closer to You so that I may hear Your voice and confess Your name wherever I go. Amen.

A Divine Schoolhouse

They read from the Book of the Law of God, making it clear and giving the meaning so that the people understood what was being read.

NEHEMIAH 8:8

As God's house is a house of prayer, prayer should inspire everything that is done there. Prayer belongs to every sort of work relating to the church. As God's house is a house of prayer, so it is also a place where shaping praying people out of prayerless people is done.

The house of God is a divine schoolhouse, in which the lesson of prayer is taught, where men and women learn to pray, and where they graduate from the school of prayer.

GOD, in Your House, do we learn the art of praying. Thank You for revealing more of You through Your Word. Amen.

144

ANTI-MISSIONARY

"You will receive power when the Holy Spirit comes on you; and you will be My witnesses in Jerusalem, and in all Judea and Samaria, and to the ends of the earth."

ACTS 1:8

An anti-missionary Christian is a contradiction, as it is impossible to be so. It is impossible for the divine and human forces to put people in such a position not to align them with the missionary cause.

Missionary impulse is the heartbeat of our Lord Jesus Christ sending His own vital forces through the whole body of the church. When these life forces die down, then death follows. Likewise, anti-missionary churches are dead churches, just as anti-missionary Christians are dead Christians.

LORD, ignite the fires of enthusiasm, passion and fervor in my heart so that I will bring You glory. Amen.

145

A Missionary Age

For Christ's love compels us, because we are convinced that one died for all, and therefore all died.
2 CORINTHIANS 5:14

We are living in a missionary age. The missionary movement has grown to awaken hope and ignite enthusiasm in the coldest and most lifeless people.

The danger, however, is that the missionary movement will move ahead of the missionary spirit. This has always been the danger of the church—losing the substance in the shade, losing the spirit, and being satisfied with proclaiming the movement, but not putting the spirit in the movement.

GOD, I pray today for all the missionaries out there spreading the gospel. Guide them, protect them and bless them with Your abundant blessings. Amen.

Private Prayer in Public Worship

Let everything that has breath praise the Lord.
PSALM 150:6

God's house is a holy place for united worship. A quiet room is for individual prayer. Yet even in the house of God, there is the element of private worship.

God's people are to worship Him and pray to Him personally, even in public worship. The church is for the united prayer of God's family, but also for individual believers.

The life, power and glory of the church is prayer. The life of its members is dependent on prayer. The presence of God is secured and retained by prayer. The very place is made sacred by its ministry. Without it, the church is lifeless and powerless.

LOVING FATHER, I want to pray to You on all occasions with all kinds of prayers and requests by the help of Your Spirit. Amen.

Money or Prayer?

And my God will meet all your needs according to the riches of His glory in Christ Jesus.

PHILIPPIANS 4:19

Many of us have heard earnest speeches stressing the need of money for missions while we have heard perhaps a few stressing the need of prayer.

The common idea among church leaders is that if we get the money, prayer will come. The very opposite is actually true. If we get the church involved in praying, and thus secure the spirit of missions, money will more than likely come as a matter of course.

Spiritual duties and spiritual factors left to the "matter of course" law, will surely die down. Only the things that are stressed live and rule in the spiritual realm.

FATHER GOD, thank You for the knowledge and certainty that You will meet all our needs abundantly. We only need to ask and pray. Amen.

Born in the Divine Mind

"I am going to send you what My Father has promised; but stay in the city until you have been clothed with power from on high."

LUKE 24:49

Missions mean the bringing of the Gospel to those who have never heard of Christ. It means giving to others the opportunity to hear of salvation through our Lord Jesus Christ, and allowing others to have a chance to receive and accept the blessings of the Gospel.

It means that those who enjoy the benefits of the Gospel give these same religious advantages and Gospel privileges to all of mankind. Prayer has a great deal to do with missions.

Both prayer and missions were born in the Divine Mind. Prayer creates and makes missions successful, while the success of missions leans heavily on prayer.

LORD, I want to spread the Good News so that others can also have the chance to receive salvation. Amen.

149

Praying Creates a Giving Spirit

Yet for us there is but one God, the Father, from whom all things came and for whom we live; and there is but one Lord, Jesus Christ, through whom all things came and through whom we live.

1 CORINTHIANS 8:6

The people who give will not necessarily pray. One of the evils of the present-day missionary movement lies just there. Giving is removed from prayer. Prayer receives little attention, while giving stands out. Those who truly pray will be moved to give. Praying creates a giving spirit. The praying ones will give liberally and self-denyingly. He who prays to God will also open his purse to God. But mechanical, reluctant giving kills the very spirit of prayer.

ALMIGHTY GOD, I pray that You will open my eyes and my heart to people in need of material and spiritual things. Amen.

150

THE GRACE OF GIVING

For Zion's sake I will not keep silent, for Jerusalem's sake I will not remain quiet, till her vindication shines out like the dawn, her salvation like a blazing torch.

ISAIAH 62:1

It is truly astonishing how great a part money plays in the modern religious movements and how little part prayer plays.

In striking contrast with that statement, it is marvelous what small part money played in early Christianity as a factor in spreading the Gospel, and how wonderful a part prayer played in it. The grace of giving is nowhere refined more than spending quiet time with God in prayer.

The spreading of Christ's Kingdom lies in regular prayer, and not in the offering box.

HEAVENLY FATHER, I realize again today, that prayer can change things. Our prayers move You, Lord. Let money not become too important in my life; I want You in first place. Amen.

151

QUANTITY OR QUALITY MEMBERSHIP?

"Who is blind but my servant?"

ISAIAH 42:19 RSV

There is a blindness in the church with regard to members choosing a life of sin over God's way of life.

The truth is, there is such a lust for members in the church, that the officials have entirely lost sight of the members who are living in open disregard of God's Word. The idea now is quantity in membership, not quality. Prayer can change this. Through prayer, members would either confess their sins, or leave the church.

GOD, I pray that You will open the eyes of Your people. Especially those in leadership positions in Your church so that they will focus more on quality than quantity of members. Amen.

152

Fitness in Prayer

For physical training is of some value, but godliness has value for all things, holding promise for both the present life and the life to come.

1 TIMOTHY 4:8

If you are not a praying man here at home you need to develop fitness in prayer in order to become a missions worker abroad.

If you are not compassionate towards people around you, how can you have compassion for people abroad? Missionaries are not believers who are failures at home. A person must first be a person of prayer at home before becoming a missionary and pray overseas.

In other words, it takes the same spiritual qualifications for being a home missions worker as it does for being a foreign missions worker.

FATHER GOD, wherever I am, be it at my home or somewhere abroad, I need to be a missionary for You. Guide me in this task through Your Spirit. Amen.

153

God's Called People

"Ask the Lord of the harvest, therefore, to send out workers into His harvest field."

MATTHEW 9:38

God in His own way, in answer to the prayers, calls believers to His harvest fields. People should be called to be missionaries. They must not just feel obliged to go because of pressure from their church or missionary board. They must be chosen by God.

Is the harvest great? Are the laborers few? Pray! Oh, that a great wave of prayer would sweep over the church, asking God to send out laborers into the needy harvest fields!

There is no danger of the Lord sending out too many laborers and crowding the fields. If He calls you, He will equip you.

DEAR GOD, help us not to send people to the harvest field independent of Your call. We only need to pray, You will prepare Your workers. Amen.

Faith That God Is Able

"When the Son of Man comes, will He find faith on the earth?"

LUKE 18:8

The possibilities of prayer are measured by faith in God's ability to do. Faith is the one prime condition by which God works and is the one prime condition by which man prays.

Faith believes in God's limitless power. Faith gives character to prayer. A feeble faith has always brought forth feeble praying. Vigorous faith creates vigorous praying. We need a quickening faith in God's power.

We have restricted God to fit into our world, and now we have little faith in His power. We have made Him a little God through our little faith.

GOD, I pray that You will increase my faith in Your ability to accomplish anything. What is impossible for man is possible with You. Glory to Your name. Amen.

155

The History of Prayer

Trust in the LORD and do good; dwell in the land and enjoy safe pasture.

PSALM 37:3

The possibilities of prayer are established by the facts and the history of prayer. Facts are stubborn things. Facts are true things.

Theories may be but speculations. Opinions may be wrong. But facts are reliable. They cannot be ignored. What are the possibilities of prayer judged by the facts? What is the history of prayer? What does it reveal to us? Prayer has a history, written in God's Word and recorded in the experiences and lives of God's saints.

History is truth teaching by example. We may miss the truth by perverting the history, but the truth is in the facts of history.

FATHER, thank You that there is proof in Your Word of the possibilities and power of prayer. Thank You that I can know the Truth, and that the Truth sets me free. Amen.

God and History

Commit your way to the Lord; trust in Him and He will do this: He will make your righteous reward shine like the dawn, your vindication like the noonday sun.

PSALM 37:5-6

God reveals Himself through the facts of religious history. God teaches us His will by the facts and examples of Bible history. God has ruled the world by prayer and He still rules the world in the same divinely ordained way.

The possibilities of prayer cover not only individuals but also cities and nations. The praying of Moses was the one thing that stood between the wrath of God against the Israelites, and the execution of that divine purpose.

Nineveh was saved because the king and its people repented of their evil ways and gave themselves to prayer and fasting.

FATHER, through the facts of religious history in the Bible we can learn much about Your character. I praise Your name. Amen.

157

God's Will Be Done

Let the message of Christ dwell among you richly as you teach and admonish one another...singing to God with gratitude in your hearts.

COLOSSIANS 3:16

God's Word is a record of prayer—of praying people and their achievements. No one can read the instances, commands, and examples of statements that concern themselves with prayer, without realizing that the cause of God and the success of His work in this world are committed to prayer.

A reverence for God's holy name is closely related to a high regard for His Word. This hallowing of God's name, the ability to do His will on earth as it is done in heaven, and the establishment and glory of God's Kingdom are as much involved in prayer as when Jesus taught men the Lord's Prayer.

DEAR GOD, I realize that much of the successes in my life depend on my prayers to You. Thank You for the gift of prayer. Amen.

Midway Between God and Man

During the days of Jesus' life on earth, He offered up prayers and petitions with fervent cries and tears.
HEBREWS 5:7

True prayer links itself to the will of God and runs in streams of compassion and intercession for all people.

As Jesus Christ died for all people so prayer gives itself for the benefit of all people. Like our Mediator between God and people, he who prays stands midway between God and people.

Prayer holds the movements of believers in its grasp and embraces the destinies of believers for all eternity. It touches heaven and moves earth. Prayer connects earth to heaven and brings heaven in close contact with earth.

FATHER, thank You that true praying links us to Your will. Thank You that it can touch heaven and move earth. Amen.

159

GOD'S RECIPE FOR PRAYER

Through faith...gained what was promised.

HEBREWS 11:33

Under certain circumstances, persistent prayer can bring additional assurance of God's promises. There would seem to be the capacity in prayer for going beyond the Word, beyond His promise, and into the very presence of the Father Himself.

Jacob wrestled, not so much with a promise as with the Promiser. We must take hold of the Promiser, or else the promise is without purpose. Prayer may well be defined as the force that vitalizes and energizes the Word of God, by taking hold of God Himself. By taking hold of the Promiser, prayer releases the personal promise.

GOD, thank You that You are always faithful to Your promises. Amen.

160

Prayer Privileges

Seek the Lord while He may be found; call on Him while He is near. Let the wicked forsake their ways and the unrighteous their thoughts. Let them turn to the Lord, and He will have mercy on them, and to our God, for He will freely pardon.

ISAIAH 55:6-7

As there is no difference in the kind of sin people find themselves in, everybody needs the saving grace of God.

Further, as this saving grace is obtained only in answer to prayer, people are therefore called to pray because of their very needs.

It is a privilege for every follower of God to pray, but it is also a duty for him to call upon God. God shows mercy to all sinners. All are welcome to approach the throne of grace with all their wants and needs; with all their sins and burdens.

FATHER GOD, thank You for the great privilege of prayer. But I also know that as a Christian it is my duty to pray. Thank You for Your mercy and grace. Amen.

Blessed to Bless

"Very truly I tell you, whoever believes in Me will do the works I have been doing, and they will do even greater things than these, because I am going to the Father."

JOHN 14:12

Prayer joined with loving obedience is the answer to all ends and all things. Prayer joined to the Word of God makes all God's gifts sacred.

Prayer is not simply to receive things from God, but to make those things holy that have already been received from Him. It is not merely to receive a blessing, but also to be able to give a blessing. Prayer makes common things holy and worldly things sacred.

Prayer receives things from God with thanksgiving and hallows them with thankful hearts and devoted service.

ALMIGHTY GOD, I thank You, that prayer and loving obedience are the answer to all things in this life. I praise You for all the blessings received from Your hand. Amen.

162

GOD'S WORD IN OUR HEARTS

For everything God created is good, and nothing is to be rejected if it is received with thanksgiving, because it is consecrated by the word of God and prayer.

1 TIMOTHY 4:4-5

God's good gifts are holy, not only because of God's creative power, but because they are made holy by prayer.

Doing God's will is essential for effectual praying. You may ask, how are we to know what God's will is? By studying His Word and by letting the Word dwell in us richly. It shows us that we cannot only do the will of God externally, but from the heart, without holding back from the intimate presence of the Lord.

LORD, by meditating on Your Word and keeping it in our hearts, we can know what Your will is. I want to be in Your presence constantly, so that I can do Your will. Amen.

163

FILLED WITH GOD'S SPIRIT

He is always wrestling in prayer for you, that you may stand firm in all the will of God, mature and fully assured.

COLOSSIANS 4:12

To know God's will in prayer, we must be filled with God's Spirit, who intercedes for the saints.

To be filled with God's Spirit and to be filled with God's Word, is to know God's will. It is to be put in such a state of heart that it will enable us to read and correctly interpret the purposes of the eternal.

Filling our hearts with the Word and the Spirit gives us an insight into the will of the Father. It enables us to discern His will and to make it the guide and compass of our lives.

GOD, my prayer today is to be filled with Your Spirit, so that I may know Your will. You are the guide and compass of my life. Amen.

164

THE UNIVERSALITY OF PRAYER

May the God of hope fill you with all joy and peace as you trust in Him, so that you may overflow with hope by the power of the Holy Spirit.

ROMANS 15:13

Prayer has far-reaching and worldwide effects. Prayer goes everywhere and lays its hand upon everything. There is a universality in prayer.

Prayer is individual in its application and benefits, but it is general and worldwide at the same time in its good influences. Prayer blesses man in every event of life, provides help in every emergency, and gives comfort in every trouble.

There is no experience that people need to face without prayer as a helper, a comforter, and a guide.

FATHER, thank You for the great gift of prayer. We can face every situation in life through our prayers to You. You will answer us and comfort us. Amen.

165

SCRIPTURAL AUTHORITY

Faith comes from hearing the message, and the message is heard through the word about Christ.

ROMANS 10:17

By scriptural authority, prayer may be divided into the petition of faith and that of submission. The prayer of faith is based on the written Word, for it inevitably receives its answer—the very thing for which it prays.

The prayer of submission is without a definite word of promise, so to speak. But it takes hold of God with a remorseful spirit and pleads with Him for that which the soul desires.

Abraham had no definite promise that God would spare Sodom. But he gained his plea with God when he interceded for the Israelites with persistent prayers and many tears.

FATHER, through persistent prayers and many tears Abraham interceded for the Israelites and gained his plea. Thank You that You always hear our prayers and will answer them in good time. Amen.

166

Call on God's Name

For there is no difference...the same Lord is Lord of all and richly blesses all who call on Him.

ROMANS 10:12

When we speak of the universality of prayer, we discover many sides to it. First, it is important that all people should pray.

Prayer is intended for all people, because all people need God and need what God has and what only prayer can give. As people are called upon to pray everywhere, they need to pray for others everywhere.

Universal terms are used when believers are commanded to pray. There is a promise in universal terms to all who call upon God for pardon, for mercy and help.

LOVING FATHER, I praise You, for the knowledge we have that we can pray to You anywhere and at any time. Amen.

167

The Prayer Environment

I want the men everywhere to pray, lifting up holy hands without anger or disputing.

1 TIMOTHY 2:8

God's children can pray everywhere, since God is accessible in every climate and under all circumstances. There is just one modification of this idea.

Some places exist in which evil business is conducted. The intrinsic environments of these settings grow out of the places, out of the moral character of those who do business there, and out of those who support them. In such places, prayer would not be appropriate.

Prayer is so much out of place at such places that no one would ever presume to pray there.

GOD, thank You for being accessible to us in every climate and under all circumstances. But make us aware of the fact that prayer is more appropriate in some places than others. Amen.

168

Where to Pray

"I have the right to do anything," you say—but not everything is beneficial. "I have the right to do anything"—but I will not be mastered by anything.

1 CORINTHIANS 6:12

While we are to pray everywhere, it means that we should not visit places where we cannot pray. To pray everywhere is to pray in all legitimate places, and to attend especially those places where prayer is welcome. To pray everywhere is to preserve the spirit of prayer in places of business, in our dealings with people, and in the privacy of the home.

The model prayer of our Lord is the universal prayer because it is adapted to all people everywhere and in all times of need.

LORD, I want to thank You for giving us an example in Your Word of how we ought to pray. Amen.

Those in Authority

I urge, then, first of all, that petitions, prayers, intercession and thanksgiving be made for all people— for kings and all those in authority, that we may live peaceful and quiet lives in all godliness and holiness.

1 TIMOTHY 2:1-2

It is especially important to pray regularly for our church leaders. It makes good rulers, and makes good rulers better rulers. It restrains the lawless and the despotic. Rulers are to be prayed for. They are not out of reach and control of prayer, because they are not out of reach and control of God.

Wicked Nero was on the throne of Rome when Paul wrote these words urging prayer for those in authority.

GOD, I pray today for all the people in leadership positions all over the world that they will know and follow You as the divine Leader and King. Amen.

170

Vital Force of Prayer

"If you believe, you will receive whatever you ask for in prayer."

MATTHEW 21:22

Unless the power of prayer is supplied by God's Word, prayer, though earnest, is empty.

The absence of power in praying can be traced to the absence of a constant supply of God's Word to repair the waste and renew the life. He who wants to learn to pray well must first study God's Word and store it in his memory and thoughts.

When we consult God's Word, we find that no duty is more binding than that of prayer. No promises are more radiant, more abounding, than those that are attached to prayer.

FATHER GOD, I know that I can only learn to pray well by studying Your Word and keeping it in my heart. I want to fulfill the great duty I have of being Your praying servant. Amen.

171

Big-Hearted Prayers

The Lord upholds all who are falling and raises up all who are bowed down.

PSALM 145:14 RSV

Compassion should be present in our hearts when we pray and people should engage their thoughts in approaching the throne of grace.

No man with narrow views of God, of His plan to save people, and of the universal needs of all people can pray effectively. It takes a broad-minded man who understands God and His purposes in the Atonement to pray well.

Prayer comes from a big heart, filled with thoughts about and sympathies for all people.

GOD, I know that it takes a broad-minded and big-hearted person who knows Your will to pray well. Please guide me in becoming more like Jesus every day. Amen.

172

Prayer Brings Heaven to Earth

"I have told you these things, so that in Me you may have peace. In this world you will have trouble. But take heart! I have overcome the world."

JOHN 16:33

Prayer runs parallel with the will of God. Prayer reaches up to heaven and brings heaven down to earth. Prayer contains a double blessing.

It rewards the person who prays and blesses him who is prayed for. It brings peace to places of conflict. There is an inner and outer calm that comes to him who prays.

Right praying not only makes life beautiful and peaceful, but it also infuses righteousness. Honesty, integrity and strength of character are the natural and essential fruit of prayer.

LORD GOD, thank You that in You we may have peace. I know that trouble will come my way, but I also know that I need not fear because You have already overcome the world. Amen.

173

Our Great Intercessor

Praise be to the God and Father of our Lord Jesus Christ, the Father of compassion and the God of all comfort, who comforts us in all our troubles, so that we can comfort those in any trouble with the comfort we ourselves receive from God.

2 CORINTHIANS 1:3-4

Worldwide, selfless praying pleases God and is acceptable in His sight, because it co-operates with His will and runs in gracious streams to God's people.

It is this kind of praying that Christ Jesus did when He was on earth, and the same kind that He is now doing at His Father's right hand in heaven as our mighty Intercessor.

He is the pattern of prayer. He stands between God and man, the one Mediator who gave Himself as a ransom for each and every person.

LORD, thank You for loving us so much that You gave Your only Son so that we could live with You eternally in heaven. Amen.

174

THE HOUSE OF PRAYER

"If you remain in Me and My words remain in you, ask whatever you wish, and it will be done for you."
JOHN 15:7

As God's house is called the house of prayer because prayer is the most important of its tasks, so the Bible also may be called the Book of prayer. Prayer is the great theme of the Bible's message to mankind.

As the Word of Christ dwells richly in us, we become transformed. The result is that we become praying Christians.

Faith is constructed of the Word and the Spirit, and faith is the body and substance of prayer. His Word becomes the basis of and the inspiration for our praying.

LORD, You say that if we remain in You and Your Word remains in us, we may ask whatever we wish, and it will be given to us. I praise Your holy name for being so good to us. Amen.

175

The Endless Possibilities of Prayer

Now to Him who is able to do immeasurably more than all we ask or imagine.

EPHESIANS 3:20

Paul, in his remarkable prayer for the Ephesians, honored the unlimited possibilities of prayer, and he glorified the ability of God to answer prayer.

Prayer is all-inclusive. There is no time or place that prayer does not cover and sanctify. All things on earth and in heaven, everything for time and for eternity, all are embraced in prayer.

Nothing is too great and nothing is too small to be a subject of prayer. Prayer reaches down to the least things of life and includes the greatest things that concern us.

DEAR HEAVENLY FATHER, I thank You that I can pray to You about anything. Nothing is too great and nothing is too small to bring to You in prayer. Amen.

A Cure for Undue Care

Do not be anxious about anything, but in every situation, by prayer and petition, with thanksgiving, present your requests to God. And the peace of God, which transcends all understanding, will guard your hearts and your minds in Christ Jesus.

PHILIPPIANS 4:6-7

Worry is the epidemic evil of mankind. Everybody is influenced by worry.

There are the cares of the home, from which there is no escape except in prayer. There are the cares of business, the cares of poverty, and the cares of riches. We live in a fearful world, and we are a fearful race. The caution of Paul is well addressed in Philippians 4:6-7. This is the divine command, so that we might be able to live above anxiety and freed from undue care.

This is the divinely prescribed remedy for all anxiety, all worry, and all troubles.

LORD, I know that we can bring our cares and burdens to You. You will give us comfort and rest because You care for us. Amen.

177

LIVING WORRY-FREE

The peace of God, which transcends all understanding, will guard your hearts.

PHILIPPIANS 4:7

Only prayer can bring the "peace of God, which transcends all understanding" into the heart and mind (Phil. 4:7).

Cares divide, distract, bewilder, and destroy unity and quietness of mind. What great need to guard against them and learn the one secret of their cure—prayer! Prayer about everything can quiet every distraction, and lift every care from weary lives and from confused hearts.

The specific prayer is the perfect cure for all anxieties, cares, and worries. Only prayer can drive worry away and save from worrying over things that we cannot change.

FATHER, I bring all my worries and anxieties to You today. I leave them at Your feet. Please give me peace. In Jesus' name I pray. Amen.

178

The Key of Missionary Success

"For the Son of Man came to seek and to save the lost."

LUKE 19:10

If Satan cannot prevent a great movement for God, his craftiest trick is to try to ruin the movement. Only mighty prayer will save the movement from being materialized and keep the spirit of the movement strong and alive.

The key of all missionary success is prayer. That key is in the hands of the churches. Financial resources are not the real muscles of war in this fight. Machinery carries no power to break down heathen walls and win heathen hearts to Christ.

Prayer alone can accomplish this.

FATHER GOD, the key to all missionary success lies in our prayers rising up to You. Guide us and strengthen us to keep on praying even when words fail us. Amen.

179

Rejoice Always

Rejoice in the Lord always. I will say it again: Rejoice! Let your gentleness be evident to all. The Lord is near.

PHILIPPIANS 4:4-5

In a world filled with all kinds of worry, where temptation is the rule, where there are so many things testing us, how is it possible to rejoice all the time?

We look at the command to rejoice always, and we accept it and respect it as the Word of God, but no joy comes. We decide to be kind and gentle. We remember the nearness of the Lord, but still we are hasty, quick and impatient.

A joyous, carefree, peaceful experience brings the believer into a joyous living by faith. We should only obey and trust God.

FATHER, in this broken world we live in, it is difficult to rejoice always. But I know that to live according to Your will, my life will be a joyful experience pleasing in Your sight. Amen.

180

PRAYER THAT GETS ANSWERS

When you ask, you do not receive, because you ask with wrong motives, that you may spend what you get on your pleasures.

JAMES 4:3

Answers to prayer are the only surety we have that we prayed right. What marvelous power there is in prayer! What untold miracles it works in this world! Why is it that the average prayer goes begging for an answer? God is not playing make-believe in His marvelous promises to answer prayer.

The whole explanation is found in our wrong prayers. We ask and do not receive because we ask wrong. Child of God, can you pray? If not, why not? Answered prayer is the proof of your real praying.

FATHER, when I do not receive an answer to my prayers, let me examine my own motives. Guide me through Your Spirit to pray with an honest and sincere heart. Amen.